THE

DESTRUCTION

OF

CITY

TATTERSALLS

THE DESTRUCTION OF CITY TATTERSALLS

By
Tweedledum
And
Tweedledee

Johny Bineham

THE
DESTRUCTION
OF
CITY
TATTERSALLS
By
Tweedledum
And
Tweedledee

Copyright © Johny Bineham

This book is copyright. Subject to statuary exceptions and to the provisions of relevant collective licencing agreements. No reproductions may take place without the written agreement of Johny Bineham.

Johny Bineham, Sydney, New South Wales,
Australia.
isbn
ISBN-13: 978-1495489112
ISBN-10: 1495489116

First published 2014

By Tweedledum And Tweedledee

Dedication

This book is dedicated to the many friends I've met over many years at Sydney City Tattersalls Club, especially those wonderful friends who frequented the Celebrity Room of the Club for Ballroom Dancing.

Also, a special mention to all those decent hardy souls everywhere, but especially those at City Tattersalls Club, who have been prepared to continually stand up against mismanagement and incompetence - no matter what the personal cost.

Contents

Preface			i
Introduction			9
Chapter	1	Why Tweedledum?	20
Chapter	2	Tatts Mortgage	37
Chapter	3	Tatts Elections	46
Chapter	4	Ode	55
Chapter	5	Proposed High Rise	61
Chapter	6	Vision for Tatts	74
Chapter	7	Dance at Tatts	86
Addendum	A	Tatts Forum	92
Addendum	B	Club Rules	145
Addendum	C	Committee	149
Addendum	D	Distribution	150
Addendum	E	Other Books	156

By Tweedledum And Tweedledee

"When a well packaged web of lies has been sold gradually to the masses over generations, the truth will seem utterly preposterous and its speaker a raving lunatic."
    Dresden james

"Ignorance is the softest pillow on which a man can rest his head"
    Michel de Montaigne

INTRODUCTION

From the heart of the fountain of delight rises a jet of bitterness that tortures us among the very flowers.
    Lucretius

Waking up and standing up.

This book is about waking up and standing up to those who use underhand and deceitful measures to get their own way at City Tattersalls.
  This book is also a tale of woe, so bad that I had to write it in a satirical manner otherwise if you were reading it over dinner, you would be crying in your soup - and I wouldn't want that.

Doing research for this book, I asked quite a few Members what they thought, first of the CEO Tony Guilfoyle, then the Chairman Patrick Campion. Now I couldn't get any comments on the Committee members because there was so much invective, blasphemies and foul language about the CEO and the Chairman, that a maiden wouldn't understand and an older lady would faint, so much so, that the poor old Committee missed entirely out on any commentary. I knew there were many, many angry Members but I had no idea as to what degree. Really, the CEO and the Chairman can count themselves lucky that Lynch Law is outlawed.

This book is a also a morality tale illustrating just what can happen to a great financially successful Club that was professionally run and brim full of Members, around 30,000, when it it was taken over and literally raped and pillaged for the benefit of a few but especially one person. He, the CEO, has been allowed to literally run amok like a mad prince and do whatever whim took his fancy at the time, all allowed by compromised Chairmen and mainly weak sycophantic Committee Members.

Well it all could be coming to a head spurred on by the possibility of a 48 storey high rise building heading skywards with the millions involved. City Tattersalls nowadays is becoming more and more newsworthy because of current and ongoing investigations being carried out by various state authorities.

Some are predicting the crud will hit the fan in 2014. We shall see. Meanwhile, the Chairman and the Committee have just renewed the CEO's contract. I believed they waited until Committee persons who might oppose it were away allowing a meeting to be fast tracked with the necessary numbers.

This book, notwithstanding its satirical flavour and amusing art-work, endeavours to give an open account of the Club's little known mismanagement. What has been written down about the goings-on at the Club has been in the public domain on internet for many months, some for even years.

Of course amongst the book's satirical conjecturing, imaginings, suppositions and inconclusive conclusions, there may be found some misgivings, some inaccuracies, but nothing written herein, is intentionally malevolent or dishonest, even and although, by drawing attention to the magnitude of the Club's misguided management, it may appear to have it leaning in that direction.

There is nothing within this book that should not be out in the open and known, but unfortunately, management has kept vital information from the Members, the very people who are entitled to know, realise, understand and comprehend.

If the the Club was run openly and transparently there would be no need for a book such as this. Unfortunately, the gross secrecy and deception coming from the Management and Committee has created the necessity for disclosure.

This book lays out before Members, an exposé of the enormity of unfair and unethical business practices conducted at City Tattersalls. The booklet's intention is to let Members know, who otherwise have no way of knowing, to what degree their Club has been mismanaged.

Over the years at City Tattersalls, the Executive 'Tail' has at will and in any direction, wagged the elected 'Dog' Committee. This ludicrous situation has allowed some Executive Staff to be paid huge monetary bonuses while those workers at the coal face, actually making the money, have had even their traditional and princely annual $100 bonuses not paid for some five years.

This is not just immoral and unethical, it is grossly unfair when extraordinary, extravagant and excessively huge salaries and bonuses are paid by the executives to the executives. A disgruntled former Club employee expressed his disgust with the comment, "They're grubs!"

It is patently obvious that no matter how hard one tries to be dispassionate and honest in presenting this information, when the Club is run like a secret society at the Executive and Committee levels, there is bound to be some inaccuracies. Some information is suppositional and conjectural, simply because of the 'closed shop' mentality of the Committee and

Management, leaves one no choice. For instance, not once has a Committee person ever replied to any of my letters even though personally addressed to them.

Also presented to the reader is the information in the public arena on the internet: the *Save City Tatts,* and the *City Tattersalls Members Forum*, all in the public domain. Some savecitytatts allegations are strong stuff indeed, but nowhere do I see refutations of those exposures, even though comments or rebuttals are invited.

As or myself, my material possessions in this world are minor, no car or house to call my own (tears), but I do have my good name having won it over a lifetime of fighting for various causes including three stints on Active Service in three wars. My good name and reputation, I was advised by my dear departed friend John Traill, Q.C., were valued in law up to $2,000,000, should it ever be defamed by another.

Now, should others, by their actions, not have those standards for their name and reputation, by vigorously refuting untruths that are uttered or printed, well that's their business.

Of course, defamation and libel laws are useless when the information presented is the truth. John Traill also advised me that it is too late to be shocked at some allegation six months or a year after it has become common knowledge.

The aim of this booklet is to also air publicly the current situation at City Tatts, such as all the Club assets and its freehold being mortgaged in their entirety.

Instead of a blunt admission in plain English, the Members have only been given some partial particulars by the Chairman in the Club's Quarterly Magazine.

For the first time in the Club's financially fine history, a bank now has its claws dug deep into all the commercial assets of City Tattersalls, however, the CEO, the Chairman and the Committee, aren't telling - hence this book. A book which is intended to shine a little light into the secret dark recesses that makes up City Tattersalls at present.

I also find it intriguing that Colliers who acted for Merivale in its sale of the Merivale Building (194 Pitt Street), to City Tatts in 2004 for $9,000,000 through the NAB, had as a part of its contract 'that it can't be renovated for five years'. In fact no D.A. was ever put into the Council for approval.

Ho hum - you might say, I might even agree that it certainly 'hums', but the good thing about having Colliers now acting for the sale of the City Tatts Club's high rise, with its most likely sale to Mirvac, is that it saves time; and 'time is money' you know.

The real charm of these 'revolving door' situations is that everybody already knows each other, which avoids wasting valuable time on tenders and such like.

It would be an interesting exercise to see a list of the disbursements, the various break-downs, of the $9 million sale from 194 Pitt Street to Merivale. It would make for interesting reading with such fascinating characters and well thought out plot.

What's my personal agenda in writing this book?
It's no vendetta or seeking personal satisfaction monetary or otherwise, I simply want to see Tattersalls once more be the great Club that it once used to be. A Club that I and other Members can be truly proud to be a Member of. A Club where I can take my friends to with pride. It certainly has the potential, it just needs the necessary leadership.

I readily admit the impetus for writing this book was a number of broken promises made to me on various occasions by CEO Tony Guilfoyle and on one specific occasion by the Chairman, Patrick Campion. The promises and assurances were about improving the Club by getting more Members and guests to the dancing venues by improving its present dismal and dull dances (Thankfully though, the quarterly formal Dinner Dances continue to be a success).

The other assurances was that they would advertise the social activities and the sub-Clubs on the frontage, or in the foyer, to allow Members, guests and overseas visitors, but especially the 200,000 of weekly passing trade who haven't a clue what is going on inside apart from the pokies. Break your personal promises to me, well I just don't cop it sweet, no sir, instead you get a book that will never go away.

However, I now realise full well, that by not improving the dance scene is but one more facet of their strategy to run the Club down financially, so that there is no remaining option but to sell the high rise to 'save' the Club.

This is why anything that might improve the Club's finances is viewed with deep suspicion by the CEO and the Chairman. As is anything that might thwart their personal secret agenda and long term strategy of a city complex consisting of a Club, hotel and units rising majestically skywards to pierce any low flying clouds - City Tatts triumphant.

I personally am not against such a vision but I am definitely against having the grubby clutches of Tweedledum and Tweedledee anywhere near it unless the Club Members want future failure guaranteed.

I have been a member of City Tattersalls since 1983 - from its heydays to its present comparative 'low-days.' For those who are unaware of me, I am John Bineham, the once President of the Dance Club for ten years, which was more than enough time dealing with the Club Management.

Thankfully, I recall being a member during those high times when it was both an honour and a privilege to be a Member of such an illustrious Sydney Club, where one mixed with the best of the best.

Most, but not all of the present Committee rarely socialise for I seldom see any on them, let alone stop them for a chat.

In actual fact, the CEO, the Chairman, the Members of the Committee, should be leading by example and be at the forefront of the Club's activities. Sure, regards the Committee Members - some of those hoity toity do make an effort to socialise with we, the hoi polloi - but most don't.

An excerpt from the book, City Tattersalls Club, 75 Years:
City Tattersalls Act of Parliament, of 1912
Our own Act of Parliament:

City Tattersails, Tattersalls Sydney, and Tattersalls Newcastle, are unique within the NSW Club structure, for they are incorporated under an Act of Parliament.

The first Act, introduced to Parliament on Thursday 7th of December, 1912, was hardly a raging political question. Hansard shows that it was put and passed without comment.

Mr. Thrower presented a petition from James Clarke, Chairman and Trustee, Louis Augustus Bourke, Trustee, John Barkel, Treasurer and Frank Walton, Secietary, of City Tattersalls Club, praying for leave to bring in a Bill to enable the members of City Tattersalls Club to sue and be sued in the name of its Chairman, to alter existing rules and in other respects carry out objects of the Club.

Mr. Thrower having produced the Government Gazette and The Sun Newspaper, containing the notices required by the 396th Standing Order, Petition received.

THE DESTRUCTION OF CITY TATTERSALLS

The following day, Friday, December 8th, 1912, Mr. Thrower moved pursuant to notice that leave be given to bring in the Bill — Question put and passed.

Mr. Thrower presented the Bill and a certificate of payment of the sum of 25 pounds to the credit of the Consolidated Revenue fund of the State — Bill instituted.

No fuss, no complications, yet this act, fathered by men with the gift of foresight, further amended by Parliament in 1935, has allowed City Tattersalls a freedom enjoyed by few other Clubs.

Clubs, other than those incorporated under the Co-operative Act (co-operative societies) or the Companies Act (limited companies) are unincorporated bodies. That is, the Club is the members, undivided by law, inseparable as far as legal action is concerned.

Recent amendments to the Liquor Act require all Clubs to become incorporated under either Act mentioned above, and in the amendments, City TattersalTs Club gained specific exclusion due to its own Act.

It is extremely unlikely that any future Club, due to these Liquor Act provisions, will be honoured by having as its cornerstone, its own Act of Parliament.

It will be a sad, sad day for New South Wales and the fair City of Sydney, if the hierarchy of City Tattersalls Club be allowed to dismiss the Club's Rules with complete and utter contempt, while they are so adept at upholding various rules at the Annual General Meeting to inhibit debate from the Members.

A Parliamentary Inquiry.

I'm neither lawyer nor politician but as the City Tattersalls Club has its own Act of Parliament, the City Tattersalls Club

By Tweedledum And Tweedledee

Act, of 1912. Then surely it follows if those Rules are knowingly and with premeditation, broken or not adhered to, then those actions must be regarded as 'contempt of Parliament', and shouldn't the wrath of Parliament be brought down those (the CTC Chairman and those on the Committee who voted in the affirmative) who by their actions have shown blatant disrespect to the Parliament of NSW?

I, commonsense and decency, certainly think so. Apart from the other nefarious goings on at the City Tattersalls Club, shouldn't the above argument be sufficient grounds for a Parliamentary Inquiry into the Club and the negation of any contracts that have been carried out without proper adherence to the Club's Rules which are enshrined as an Act of the Parliament of New South Wales.

A Parlimentary Inquiry is critical before contracts are signed for the 48 story high-rise and multimillion dollar investment.

* There needs to be some form of NSW Parliamentary censure directed at those specific Committee Members of the City Tattersalls Club who voted in the affirmative, when they must have knowingly and specifically acted against Club Rule 6, which is a vital part of the Club Rules enacted by Parliament of 1912.

This occurred in February 2013, when the Committee resolved to borrow from the bank some of $17,540,000 without first convening a special meeting for the Members approval. Even though they each must have known that the total amount of any mortgage could not exceed $5,500,000 according to Rule 6 of the Act.

The specific Committee Members who voted to borrow $17 million by mortgaging the entire Club including its freehold, need to be named and shamed for they are a disgrace. Their actions were also kept secret from the Members in order to prevent them being voted off the Committee that same year.

* An inquiry into the "lack of duty of care" which allowed a vast pool of superannuation funds to be diminished down to virtually zero. With some members losing their entire lifetime's superannuation.

* An inquiry into why of the eight Rule changes presented in February 2013, five of which weren't allowed for discussion by the Members especially Rule 4. This proposed rule would prevent the Club's Committee or employees from entering into a contract in relation to any Club property unless it was approved by members at a General Meeting.

This one would have been a major stumbling block to the Committee's property plans so they were afraid to let members even see it, never mind vote on it.

* A inquiry into the reasons why City Tattersalls Club can make annual profits of $22 to $25 million profits from the poker machines and yet arrive at continual annual losses. Are there other reasons for this apart from excessive salaries, mismanagement and poor management by the CEO.

This book is but the first salvo of other varied broadsides until City Tattersalls is again run ethically and transparently for the benefit of its Members and the people of New South Wales.

Chapter 1

Why Tweedledum and Tweedledee?

I hold it that a little rebellion, now and then, is a good thing, and as necessary in the political world as storms in the physical...It is a medicine necessary for the sound health of government.
    Thomas Jefferson

I decided the title Tweedledum and Tweedledee being a reasonable term considering the Alice in Wonderland management style of the City Tattersalls Club's hierarchy.

For instance, a reasonable person would have expectation of even a small yearly overall profit in return for the Club's grossly over-paid executive, even the miniscule modicum of a annual profit considering over $20 annual million profit from gambling alone.

But no, it is year after year of continual losses which has put the Club in dire financial jeopardy from virtually unsustainable accumulated debt. As well, even more debt is a guaranteed certainty should Tweedledum and Tweedledee continue to remain at the helm of their 'ship of disaster' instead of rightfully being a well-run 'Queen of the Seas.'

I say the above sincerely, with a complete absence of malice, while still offering a fair, reasonable, and just opinion based on present circumstances at the Club.

In point of fact, it is so patently obvious among the Club's Members that even a moron running, even a *membrum virili cranium*, could make so small fortune, not an annual loss, from the present revenue by tapping into just some the 200,000 potential customers passing by the Club front entrance each week.

Unfortunately for City Tatts, its many activities, services and amenities have been 'purposely' hidden from vast deluge of constant passing trade because of no street or foyer advertising all the social activities going on within that would benefit the Club as well as be of benefit to visitors. As well, visitors have the potential of becoming Members to benefit the Club financially.

Those of us who have to yearly balance our own personal household budgets would agree that only two morons running could fail to balance the Club's budget with an annual profit of $20,000,000 and more from the pokies, while paying no rent on the premises. Instead an occasional small profit, it has been a chronic litany of annual losses while steadily accumulating the Club's debt to around the $25,000,000 mark.

For sheer incompetent financial management this must be worth an entry in the Guinesss Book of Abysmal Records. To take the Club with its previous unassailable commercial position with a Membership of around 30,000 must surely make them the Tweedledum and Tweedledee of Club management, with Tweedledum the CEO being in a class of his own.

Regards Tweedledee, though he has only been Chairman for 'three' years, yet he has with practiced skill accelerated the Club's debt to an alarming degree with his latest signing of the Mortgage of the Club's entire assets including freehold for

THE DESTRUCTION OF CITY TATTERSALLS

$17,540,000 without advising the Members in plain English of this abominable fact.

It is fair to speculate that, it is highly unlikely he would have been elected Chairman during the Elections in May, 2013, if the Members had known he had 'without their entitled knowledge and approval' mortgaged their Club for nearly three times the amount allowed.

I am neither for nor against the proposed high-rise of 48 floors, but I am decidedly against having Tweedledum and Tweedledee in charge of such a huge undertaking and its financial future. On their present and previous commercial track record, I wouldn't have them in charge of a soup kitchen on a busy street of starving people, let alone anywhere near a complex Sydney inner-city high-rise club, hotel and apartment block. Leopards don't change their spots. A *membrum virili cranium* is a *membrum virili cranium* come what may. 'Continue to treat a scorpion as a rose, then don't be surprised if one fine day the rose jumps up and stings you'.

I don't know about you, but I take promises and assurances seriously enough to expect them to be carried out. I was assured personally on a number of occasions that the Celebrity Room would get a new DJ to play dance music that would attract customers.

At present a morgue has more going on for it than this wonderful venue. It is dim, dark and lifeless, when it could be rocking with Members and guests especially on a Saturday night when there is virtually no Ballroom Dancing in the inner-city area. Oh dear! Why are Tweedledum and Tweedledee so against Members and guests having fun and bringing money into the Club?

Even South Sydney Juniors with their smaller dance floor still has it packed with people of all ages.

So no new DJ, even though I had been assured on separate occasions by both incompetents, neither of whom stood by their promises. I had organised one DJ, Yoppy, who has his own following and students, for an interview at Tatts. He submitted his extensive resume which demonstrated at a glance that he has had years of experience in organising and conducting successful dances in the Sydney area.

I asked Yoppy how things were going after the Club had his resume for a month or more?

He told me nothing. So I rang Jan Elks, who is the CEO's secretary and general problem solver, to ask, "What's going on?"

"It's being processed, it has to go through the system," she told me. Well a year later it must be still going through some vast subterranean system because Yoppy still hasn't had any reply from the Club.

Well, things do even out. Yoppy's treatment or lack of it became the very last straw of a number of last straws in making my final decision as to whether or not to write this book. So thanks Jan, your lack of courtesy in not replying to Yoppy was the final ill-mannered gesture that spurred me on to put out this book.

This book is not some act of revenge, nor is it written because of some personal vendetta against the Club. It was written for the very reasons I personally gave to both Tweedleduma and Tweedledee, "...to let in light where there is secrecy and deceit."

In this respect it is written for the benefit of all those Members who want a Club that is run ethically, openly and transparently for the benefit of the majority not just the 'favoured few'.

Of course, past experience should have taught me that there is no way that the CEO, Tweedledum, would have a DJ livening up the Saturday nights and maybe even one Friday night at one of the best appointed Dance venues in Sydney, that is continually and unnecessarily going to waste. It is morgue dead and in dark silence instead of being filled lots of people making merry; wining, dining and dancing in the Celebrity Room - and pray tell, why isn't this so?

Because Tony can't afford any success. He is literally scared of a successful dance scene in the Club, even with any at the other sub-Club's activities, because a people packed Club making money would put in jeopardy his long-term plan to run the Club down in order to 'save' it with the sale of the high rise.

Rather than being a smart move that the Members can'r refuse, it is only a really lame duck who would want to negotiate from a position of financial weakness, where unfortunately he has now placed the Club.

The sale of the high rise and his future part in its management, is the next step up on his personal 'career path'. Unfortunately, all at the expense of, and financial destruction of City Tattersalls. His nefarious personal agenda (his famous Secret Strategic Business Plan) is to wound the Club mortally in order to save it with an 'offer the Club can't refuse' because of it's dire financial position. Namely, it's huge manufactured and unnecessary burden of debt - I'm talking some $30,000,000 owed, give or take a few million.

I have been assured, 'over the years' that not just the dancing but the social activities of the other sub-Clubs would be promoted with street frontage, or at least highly visible signage in the foyer, advertising the Club's activities going on daily and weekly - but no. They refuse to have even this most basic of Club promotion for potential Members let alone advise the existing Members of what is actually going on in the Club.

Case in point, a friend of mine when talking about Toastmasters, asked me, "Where's the closest Toastmaster's Club?"

"Right here at City Tatts." I replied.

"Well, I've been a Member for twelve years and I didn't know that!" His answer that took me by surprise for it is ludicrous that Members don't know what is going on in their own Club.

At least four years ago at a another meeting with Tweedledum, I was assured that the Club would advertise its activities in local papers to attract some of the one million residents of the CBD living in apartments, all within fifteen and twenty minutes walk from the Club. Surely an obvious commercial move when the Club is surrounded by people who are unaware of its existence. But did anything happen?

Sadly, like his other assurances - nothing at all. On other occasions I mentioned having an Art Exhibition with say $20,000 as first prize to attract visitors and guests. and make it 'acquisitive' so that the Club owns the winning painting. "A good idea." said then Chairman John Kennedy, as well as our CEO.

Well, paintings did arrive at the Club. The dozen or so on the walls cost the Club an annual rental costing the Club $50,000 plus insurance.

No - I'm not joking - check it out. This annual rental, instead of having our own exhibition, owning the paintings, while pulling in visitors and making money for the Club.

On another occasion when the Mandarin Club was closing down, I advised Tweedledum that after making an announcement at the Mandarin Club about another dance venue in the city, I could have a hundred dancers relocate to City Tattersalls when that Club closed in three weeks.

With a stunned look on his face, he burst out saying, "No, no, John, we can't rush into these things. I have this brilliant promotions lady arriving soon, then we will look into it." he actually looked shocked at suddenly having new business on the premises. I kid you not.

Instead of, "Yes, yes, and we will welcome them all for coming with a glass of champagne as a gesture," or some such thing. - but again - nothing. I know it's hard to believe anyone actually knocking back business - but Tweedledum is a class act.

Tony can't afford to have any successful venture for a financially successful Club would ruin his very own planned ruination of the business. By the way, that 'brilliant' $240,000 per annum promotions lady came and went, as have others.

To have a hundred new customers and dancers brushed aside is surely the most asinine of actions by the most incompetent of CEOs who's ever been let loose in the world of business. He's single aim is the planned hell-bent destruction of a once thriving, bustling successful Club for his very own personal agenda.

The CEO, Tweedledum

Now don't get me wrong, I am in absolute awe of Tweedledum Tony, when it comes to his own financial rewards of annual salary, yearly bonuses. As well, I'd love a quick peek at his credit card provided by the Club.

With a present salary of over $500,000, who but Tweedledum would know what other perks and spin-offs he indulges in, to give him an annual return of who knows what, for we can only guesstimate. But I dare, I challenge anyone to say that he doesn't know how to look after his own financial gains. If only he could do the same with the Club's finances we would once again have a thriving Club.

What I feel is extra mean and very petty about Tweedledum, is his own magnificence and munificence to himself compared to that the staff on the ground floor. Those downstairs at the coal-face making money for the upstairs mob, they used to receive an annual Christmas bonus of a mere and measly $100, but they haven't received a red cent as a thank you for their efforts for some five years. While in that same time he has handed to himself and some others bonuses in the thousands. As for the trips away overseas during the past years for himself and his scyophants - I won't go into that - I wouldn't want to upset my readers.

The simple fact is that had either Tweedledum and Tweedledee kept their promises or assurances to me, namely, get a new DJ and dancing in the unused Celebrity Club; had they promoted the sub-Club activities and venues such as billiards, dancing, toastmasters, etc., by placing with signage in the foyer; had they advertised the Club locally in the CBD; had they told the truth to the Members about the $17,540,000 Mortgage of the Club, etc. , I wouldn't had put pen to paper.

In other words, had they kept their word, had they ran the Club competently and professionally, as per the Rules of the Club for the benefit of its Members, then there wouldn't be a need for this book.

I take seriously my word or promise and I expect the same of others. To break your promises to me, is to cross swords with me, not always a good move.

Impugn my good name, is to immediately understand at a personal level what the libel laws are all about.

THE DESTRUCTION OF CITY TATTERSALLS

As regards both Tweedledum and Tweedledee, I wish them personally no malice, no malevolence and no grudge, in fact I truthfully and sincerely wish them both health, wealth and happiness so long as they both stay well away from the management of City Tattersalls Club which is so essential for the very health, wealth and survival of that same Club.

Tweedledum, the Person

To meet Tony Guilfoyle is to meet with the most charming of men. He is tall and handsome, as well, he looks the part of a man who knows what he is doing. He is very affable, the most agreeable of people. At the end of a private meeting, most will walk away feeling they have made progress with their Club problem.

So one waits and waits for the outcome or agreement to become action, but one finds that all one has accomplished is the actual period of waiting, for nothing eventuates except frustration. What is also standard fare, is that something or someone else is always to blame for the lack of action.

Most give up on trying to effect any change and end up accept the situation Me, I write a book. But even a book may not be good enough to have the Club Elections conducted by the Electoral Commission. Obviously, with the ballot conducted on the Club's premises the results are open to compromise rather than any guaranteed impartiality.

At present they run by a Returning Officer, an A.R.O. masquerading in his wife's name, operating out of a Post Office Box. His outrageous fees are kept under the Club's $30,000 limit for declaration to Members, by the means of Club absorbing some of the costs. The Electoral Commission's fees are far less, so costs certainly aren't the reason for not using the NSW Electoral Commission for the Club's elections.

By Tweedledum And Tweedledee

Little will happen when you have a CEO who is hidden away like a Trappist Monk from the Members in his enclosed and closeted cell of an office on the second floor; that is when he is actually in his office. I usually visit the Club five times or more each week, both by day and by night, yet I have rarely sight his presence apart from his yearly comprehensive 'pie-chart' power-point presentation at the Annual General Meeting where he superbly demonstrates that 'bull baffles brains'.

The previous CEO, who built up the Club to a membership of around 50,000 was on a gross salary of around $260,000. At present CEO might be incompetent, but he is far from stupid. He organised a starting price salary for himself as CEO of around $460,000 plus bonuses. Even with the Club's membership crashing down around him, Members deserting the Club in droves year after year, yet amazingly, he still managed to negotiate his next contract for some $500,000, plus bonuses. Even while running at a loss despite a gaming profit of over $20 million. He's a wonder.

There is a ratio of sorts to be seen here, that is: incompetence relative to salary. It is probably the first time, in the history of the Clubs in Australia, that the membership as has crashed down while the CEO's salary has rocketed up. All happening during the watch of the previous Chairmen, John Healy and John Kennedy, as well as the present Chairman Patrick Campion. What a joke - but the only one laughing is the CEO.

The Master Puppeteer

Ever since becoming the CEO of City Tattersall Club, Tony Guilfoyle, Tweedledum, has managed to have each Chairman and most of the Committee at his beck and call, dancing merrily away to Tony's tune.

He first directs the Chairman to follow on behind, then the Committee follow the Chairman, like a small conga line of sycophants.

At least the Committee and Chairman can't be accused of being 'yes men' because when the CEO says 'no', they each say - no! How does Tweedledum do it?

How is he so successful at getting otherwise apparently normal thinking men and women to do his bidding?

Ah! It's termed one's *modus operandi*, one's 'method of operations'. Tony's method of persuasion, is to compromise people one way or the other with one thing or another. It might be something that's only slightly unethical; e.g. one John and the super, and another John for gym instruction.

I've been told that Tweedledum's ladles out uncommon generosity to his inner clique His heartfelt action chokes me up because I'm positive Tony's magnanimity has come from his own hip pocket, for I'm sure he personalises any gifts by forking out his own cash for them.

But putting gifts aside, at least Tweedledum doesn't expect others to 'agree' with him so long as they don't 'disagree' with him. As well, once he has created a compliant Executive, Chairman and Committee, it's now plain sailing for the master mariner as he sets the Club adrift on the choppy seas of bank debt.

Maybe my conjecturing, my assumptions, are all wrong. It may well be that each Chairman on his watch, that is John Healy, John Kennedy and the present Pat Campion simply love this man Tweedledum, as do a voting majority of Members on the Committee.

They love him so much they agree with all of his increases in salary; they love him so much that years later when the

By Tweedledum And Tweedledee

Committee eventually found out about the $200,000 they didn't give permission for, they didn't do anything about it; they don't mind all his hefty bonuses; his continual annual losses - now ain't love grand - that kind of love, and loyalty and subservience, kinda brings a tear to one's eye.

If I am wrong, and their driving force for allowing all his peccadillos is really their love for that man, Tweedledum, then I apologise unequivocally for any of my misconceptions.

A Real Low Flyer
On refection, one would have to conclude the the CEO has graduated with honours in the art of avoidance. For he flies so low under the radar of public gaze and publicity that he is virtually invisible. I personally gave up trying to meet with him for weeks on end only to be told I would manage a phone call in around three weeks time, by his secretary Jan Elks.

Google Tony Guilfoyle and there are only negative stories about him as excerpts from newspaper articles, or on the internet. Though. I did notice one mention of him as CEO of City Tattersalls in wikipedia.

Google Images of Tony only to discover there is not one photo of him, only one of his signature. How can the CEO of a supposed great Club not be advertised, publicised, promoted, for all his 'amazing' management skills?

Where, as in 'all' other Clubs, are the CEO, Chairman, and all the Committee Members prominently displayed proudly in glossy photos for all to see?

Is there a photo of Tony Guilfoyle anywhere to be seen?
No!
Possibly a photo of the Chairman, Patrick Campion?
Yes, I did find one on Google images.
Are you beginning to envision the picture, the mental image,

that perhaps and perchance, the Committee Members don't want to be seen to be in the limelight, or in the spotlight, or in the public gaze.

If this is so, they are certainly succeeding. But if they were really doing such a great job with the Club, shouldn't it have the blaze of publicity, be publicised and acclaimed?

Why don't any of the Committee any of the Committee stand up to speak at an AGM, or anywhere else, so they can be acclaimed for their performances?

No! They're silent faceless unknowns, unbeknown to the Members. And what's more, that's just they way they like it.

The $200,000

The $200,000 that Tweeledum took from the Club in 2004, that no one knew about at the time, which includes the Club's auditors, KPNG, who stated so in writing.

However, Tweedledee states in the Club Quarterly Magasine that Tweedledum has been exonerated on any wrong doing by The Office of Gaming & Racing.

But please Tony, explain to the Members why did you take the $200,000?

If I, or someone else took $200,000 from the Club, it would be the lock-up for us - what makes you so different?

So:
- * Who authorised giving it to him?
- * Was it the Committee?
- * Was it a loan?
- * What's the interest?
- * Why wasn't it disclosed for years?
- * Why didn't the auditors know about it?
- * Will it ever be returned to the Club?
- * What's really going on?

Well, we know one thing, it wasn't the Committee that gave

you permission because they didn't know about it for some four years. Also, when it was made known to them they did nowt about it. Ah, such is the power of love.

Sydney Morning Herald's article of August 11, 2012, however discusses the $200,000 in this way:

'Although only identified in last year's (2011) audit, the financial irregularity appears to date back to about the same time Mr Guilfoyle was appointed chief executive, in 2004.

The same year, he entered into a private business venture with Richard Manasseh. The pair are co-directors of a number of companies, including Springs Resorts and Springs Management Shoalhaven, which own two resorts, in Mittagong and Nowra.

Another of Mr Manasseh's companies, VisionAds, is a long-time provider of marketing and finance consultancy services to the club.

Mr Guilfoyle said his business ventures with Mr Manasseh were "common knowledge" at the club and had the approval of the board.

Following the Herald's questions, the club engaged the law firm Bartier Perry to release the following statement:

"In 2010 the club approved a change recommended by the auditors, KPMG. This reclassified as an asset a salary sacrifice balance that had been itemised as an offset to a trade payable. The club allows executives to receive part of their total remuneration packages as expenses, offsetting leave or other entitlements."   (Please Bartier Perry, please plain English!!)

The arrangement was approved by the club's independent tax agent, the statement said'.

The Chairman Tweedledee.

Oh dear, I do feel sorry for Patrick Campion. He is being

played as a 'patsy' by that master puppeteer Tony Guilfoyle. When the 'crud hits the fan', as it eventually must, it will be Patrick Campion who will wear it. Not Tony Guilfoyle who orchestrates everyone else to do his dirty work for him.

When this 'house of cards' crashes down, it will be Guilfoyle who will walk away 'smelling like roses', as well as all cashed up, while the Chairman and his Committee will be blamed for all of his many failures.

However, the one 'big failure' of the Chairman and the Committee that they will one day become well and truly aware of, is that they they had it in their 'collective' power to vote out the CEO on to the street, by not renewing his contract.

But no, instead they re-hire him with colossal increases in salary. Oh, you poor bloody fools - poor 'patsy' Tweedledee.

The Committee.
Far be for me to discuss the Committee as I hven't spoken to most of them. I don't want to either, what's the point as their lips are sealed.
I won't discuss any of their Committee Meetings although i will give and outline of how a meeting is run.

Firstly, no one ever sees a Committee Member carry anythng into the Meeting and they carry exactly the same amout when the leave.

Standard Committee Rules and Procedures at CTC.
As laid out by the CEO and his able secretary Jan Elks.
* Do not under any circumstances bring any pencils, pens, paper, tape recorders, laptops or briefcases to the board room.
* Only gaze, look or peruse at the document laid out in front of you by Jan, until such time as she removes it from your gaze.
* Do not even think about taking notes regarding the document in front of you.

By Tweedledum And Tweedledee

* Please leave the meeting as empty-handed as when you arrived.
* Do not discuss among yourselves or with anyone else about anything that may have transpired at the meeting.
Thank you, as always, for your most obedient cooperation.
    Jan.

A New Auditor

Every time concerned Members endeavour to bring some sanity, fairness and fair play into how the Club is run, let alone allow a Member speak out, Tweedledum and Tweedledee, to protect their own interests, dismiss or rule out any actions towards equity or fairness such as petitions and rule changes.

Only in 2013, when there was to be a proposal for a new auditor, which only required a majority show of hands at the AGM, unfortunately the person to be nominated was threatened with legal action.

Though nominated by a Member he was intimidated not to stand by Tony Tweedledum, himself, an employee of City Tattersalls Club.

But why would Tweedledum do such a thing?

Very simple, they last thing he needs to have at City Tattersalls is an independent audit of the Club's books and membership.

However both Tweedledum and Tweedledee are not as crazy as they seem to be, for they are rat cunningly adept when it comes to getting their own way.

Please note, that I say this in gushing tones of admiration and in absolute awe at their gargantuan gall.

Chapter 2

City Tattersalls Club Mortgaged in its Entirety.

One of the penalties of refusing to participate in politics is that you end up being governed by your inferiors.
        Plato

During my last meeting as President of the Dance Club with the Chairman, CEO, two Architects and another Executive, I stated I would support the 48 storey high-rise only if a majority of the Members voted for it, but I would vote against it if the majority of the Members opposed it.

During of the same meeting, Tony Guilfoyle said, "John, I know I promised we would get a new DJ for the dances three years ago, I apologise for not doing so."

Tony then went on to say. "John, why can't we put the past behind us and start afresh from today?"

"That's fine by me." I replied, while at the same time pointing at the Chairman, Patrick Campion, "You also promised me, in the company of another Member of the Committee, that we would get a new DJ."

But did anything new happen over the next few months?

Yeah! You're so right - nothing - no DJ - hence this book. It was the final straw of a fair sized bale that had accumulated after ten long years of baloney, bull, crud and hot air.

Regards this book, I did state on this and other occasions to both Tweedledum and Tweedledee that I was writing a book about the Club. Patrick Campion once asked, "Why?"

"Because of the deceit, secrecy and lack of transparency. I know of no other way to let Members know what is really going on. For example, no one knows the Club is mortgaged in its entirety. I replied.

Tony Guilfoyle then stated, "Yes they do, Patrick said so in the Club Magazine."

"Yes, true," I said, "But Patrick wrote it was a 'charge' over the Club to buy more poker machines. Most people don't realise that "Charge' was a mortgage for the amount, as well the Member's permission wasn't sought. This was a typical example of the deceit and misinformation given out to the members, in consequence, a fair and reasonable reason for my book."

Patrick Campion, the Chairman, Tweedledee, in the quarterly City Tattersalls Club Magazine, May - July 2013, in his Chairman's Message, explained the $17,540,000 mortgage over the entire Clubs assets including freehold this way:

... The Committee considered it prudent to explore what other banks might offer and we received an extremely attractive proposal from ANZ Bank. This offered us lower interest rates, less restrictive covenants, improved flexibility and certainty in return for a charge over the Club's assets.

Consequently, the Committee resolved in February 2013 to transfer the Club's banking arrangements to the ANZ from the NAB.

This change has allowed us to undertake the gaming upgrade

By Tweedledum And Tweedledee

which eventually should increase revenue'.

What the Chairman failed to mention was that a 'charge' is more than a mortgage taken over tangible assets such as house and land. It is also a mortgage over all, that being everything tangible such as real estate, freehold, as well as intangible, such as debts and liens. All, meaning everything including any and all assets at the Club's Boonoona Sky Lodge in the Snowy Mountains, for the (un-authorised by the Members) sum of $17,540,000.

This mortgage, or equitable charge, was signed by Patrick Campion as Chairman, in accordance with the NSW Parliamentary Act of 1912.

The trouble is that it wasn't accordance with the City Tattersalls Club Act of 1912, for Rule 6 of that Act of 1912, states clearly and unequivocally, that a special meeting must be held for the Members consideration (approval) for a maximum of $5,500,000. Even more brazenly, for virtually three times the amount as the maximum allowed for.

I don't know under what the legal consequences are, or if there if a term for obtaining a mortgage in a manner that is without legal authority from the Club according to the applicable Rule and that said rule is an Act of Parliament.

What I do know, as far as the Members of City Tattersalls Club are concerned, that it was a wrong, underhanded, deceitful and unethical. action to be taken by the Chairman and the Committee.

So why didn't the Chairman honestly inform Club Members in his Chairman's Message, that he had mortgaged Tattersalls to the ANZ Bank for $17,540,000, as well, as not calling a special meeting to 'consider' the mortgage over all the Club's entire assets for $17.5 million, as per Rule 6 of the Club Act,
Why?

Possibly, because of the outrage of the members for not following the Rules of the Act, for such a sizeable amount.

But why?

Because he was dead scared of the consequences.

Why again?

Because he would have most likely have ruined his chances of being re-elected as Chairman, if the voting Members had known that for the first time in its illustrious history City Tatts is mortgaged to the hilt, which somewhat diminishes its lustre and takes the shine of a fine Club. A Club that was in such a financially strong position before Tweedledum and Tweedledee got their 'metaphorical' axes to it.

Why yet again?

It would hinder the chances of gaining the Member's approval for the high rise development if the true dire financial position of the Club were known.

Actually, as a solicitor, Tweedledee must be well aware of his deception to the Members of the City Tattersalls, as well as the reasons why he has not made public the charge/mortgage of $17,540.000 over our Club.

This matter has been raised in the NSW Parliament, so it is hardly a secret, even though Tweedledum and Tweedledee would like it to be.

Finally! An Admission by the Chairman.

On Tuesday 16 November 2013, the Chairman admitted to the thirty or so Members that attended that Information Night on the proposed the high-rise of 48 storeys over and above the Club, that City Tatterssall's was indeed mortgaged to the Bank for $17,540,000.

The dialogue went something like this, when I took the microphone to clarify the Club's financial situation.

Me: "I am confused. Is it true that the entire

Chairman's Message

By Tweedledum And Tweedledee

NEW BANKING ARRANGEMENTS

As you will be aware, since the global financial crisis banks have been tightening their act. The National Australia Bank (NAB), with which we had banked for many years, made it clear to us earlier this year that it intended to extend its security from a mortgage over the FHS Street to a charge over all the Club's assets.

The Committee considered it prudent to explore what other banks might offer and we received an extremely attractive proposal from ANZ Bank. They offered us lower interest rates, less restrictive covenants, improved flexibility and certainty in return for a charge over the Club's assets.

Consequently the Committee resolved in February 2009 to transfer the Club's banking arrangements to ANZ Bank from NAB. This change has allowed us to undertake the gaming upgrade much earlier. We should thank NAB for their past support.

GAMING UPGRADE

Members will have noticed some new poker machines on the gaming floor. Over the next several months, more new machines will be introduced as part of an overall fleet upgrade.

In addition to the new machines, the Club has purchased the latest in ticket out, card in/card out gaming system, bringing the very latest gaming technology to the Club. Members will have the full benefits of this in late May 2011.

AIRSPACE DEVELOPMENT UPDATE

The application for the Sydney City Council's pre-DA Advice is likely to be lodged in June 2009 rather than May 2009. You will appreciate that the application is a complex document, involving the collaboration of many different disciplines. It is, however, progressing satisfactorily and I will continue to update you on a regular basis, including at the upcoming AGM.

We will shortly be contacting key Club Members to obtain their input on behalf of the various subsidiary Clubs.

BOONDOONA SKI LODGE BOOKINGS

There are still vacancies at Boondoona Ski Lodge but be quick.

All Chalet, Skiers and Life Members have access to City Tattersalls Club Boondoona Ski Lodge located at Perisher Valley, in the beautiful Kosciuszko National Park. The Lodge is convenient for Skiers only minutes away from the Skitube Terminal, Lifts and Perisher Centre.

Book now to experience an après ski holiday for an advance value this season.

Club's assets including the freehold are mortgaged to the ANZ Bank?"

P. Campion: "No, it's not!"

Me: "Oh, then this sheet of paper I have in my pocket which states in the NSW Parliament that City Tattersalls is mortgaged to the ANZ Bank the entire Club's assets for $17,540,000 - it's not correct?"

At this point the CEO tugged on the Chairman's sleeve, to whisper something in his ear. Immediately after, the Chairman then re-stated, "Oh, I thought you said $70 million! Yes the Club has been mortgaged for $17 million."

I then went on to say, "I presume then, that you expect to sell the high-rise for whatever millions, then deduct from that amount the Club's debts including the $17 million?"

P. Campion: "Yes!"

So there we have it, a blunt admission that the entire Club including the freehold has been mortgaged for $17,540,000.

Actually, there was little to no reaction from the Members attending, so I can only presume that they didn't quite comprehend the conversation that just took place, or its enormity went over their heads, for there was no noticeable reaction from those attending.

That admission is also another good reason for the existence of this book, namely, so Members are well aware of the activities of the Club at Management and Committee level.

By Tweedledum And Tweedledee

The Mortgage amount: $17,540,000

Signature: Patrick Campion

THE DESTRUCTION OF CITY TATTERSALLS

```
66 Req:B670766 /Doc:DL AH653962  /Rev:15-Apr-2013 /Sts:OK.OK /Prt:09-May-2013 10:57 /Pgs:ALL /Seq:1 of 1
Ref:lpi:sixdre /Src:W  /WARNING: A4 Copy Supplied by LPI NSW for Conveyancing Purposes Only.
```

Form:	05M	**MORTGAGE**	
Licence:	03-10-214	New South Wales	**AH653962R**
Licensee:	Gadens Lawyers	Real Property Act 1900	

PRIVACY NOTE: Section 31B of the Real Property Act 1900 (RP Act) authorises the ... information required by this form for the establishment and maintenance of the Real Property Act Register. Section 96B RP Act requires that the Register is made available to any person for search upon payment of a fee, if any. NSW Treasury

STAMP DUTY	Office of State Revenue use only	Clnt Nu: 109163208 3490 Duty: $50 Trns No 7059872 Asst details: Col 1 $17,580,000

(A) TORRENS TITLE	1/600465
	(referred to in this mortgage as the "land")

(B) LODGED BY	Delivery Box	Name, Address or DX and Telephone	CODE
	654X	M J ARMSTRONG & CO - GADENS LLP : 131317K Reference (optional): Doc. No. AXU / 33602673	**M**

(C) MORTGAGOR	CHAIRMAN OF CITY TATTERSALL'S CLUB ABN 44 004 054 353 pursuant to section 8 of City Tattersall's Club Act of 1912 (NSW) (referred to in this mortgage as the "mortgagor")
(D)	being the registered proprietor or entitled to be the registered proprietor of the land mortgages to ANZ all the mortgagor's estate and interest in the land specified above (subject to prior encumbrances, if any). The mortgagor covenants with ANZ as follows: 1. The provisions set out in Memorandum of Common Provisions No AA455074C filed in the Department of Lands, Land and Property Information Division and any further provisions endorsed on or annexed to this mortgage are incorporated in this mortgage. 2. The mortgagor acknowledges having received a copy of the Memorandum of Common Provisions prior to executing this mortgage.
(E)	Encumbrances (if applicable): 1. 2. 3.
(F) MORTGAGEE	AUSTRALIA AND NEW ZEALAND BANKING GROUP LIMITED ABN 11 005 357 522, Australian Credit Licence Number 234527 of 20 Martin Place Sydney New South Wales **MZ**
(G)	

DATE	28 / 02 / 2013
	dd mm yyyy

Executed by Chairman of City Tattersalls Club in accordance with the City Tattersalls Club Act 1912 (NSW)
Certified correct for the purposes of the Real Property Act 1900 by the mortgagor.

I certify that the mortgagor, with whom I am personally acquainted or as to whose identity I am otherwise satisfied, signed this mortgage in my presence. [See note* below]

Signature of witness: _Allovetto_

Full Name of witness: Michael Cossetto

Address of witness: L18 133 Castlereagh St Sydney

Signature of mortgagor: _____

Patrick Campion.

Certified correct for the purposes of the Real Property Act 1900 by the person whose signature appears below.

Signature: _____

Signatory's name: CHRISTOPHER FANNING
Signatory's capacity: Solicitor for mortgagee

10491039.1 AXU ARA

* s117 RP Act requires that you must have known the signatory for more than 12 months or have sighted identifying documentation.

THE DESTRUCTION OF CITY TATTERSALLS

Chapter 3

City Tattersalls Elections

Enlighten the people generally, and tyranny and oppressions of body and mind will vanish like evil spirits at the dawn of day.
     Thomas Jeffersen

This book is a cautionary tale of what can happen to a once great club for Members when the wrong person, Tweedledum, is placed in a position which enables him to influence and manipulate every board decision in order to gain even more power, influence and personal gain.

All this at the expense of and against the wishes of the Club's Members by dictating the voting arrangements for the Annual Committee Elections in that they are not seen to be fair, above board, and transparent to all of the Members.

Members Petition.

In order to demonstrate unequivocally total fairness, transparency and impartiality, there was a petition organised by concerned Club Members to have the ballot of the elections for the Committee conducted by the Electoral Commission.

This was to ensure a fair go for all concerned. At the Electoral Commission the votes are stored securely until they are opened after the arrival of the scrutineers, not held on the

Club's premises with the outer envelopes (thereby ensuring secrecy) opened before the arrival of the scrutineers. See letter Page 54, for confirmation of this practice.

Each year both Tony Guilfoyle and Mark Cooper are appointed scrutineers by the Committee - how very cosy.

As well, check of there is a pre-count - be surprised.

The most important point is that there should be no hint of malpractice with the Club's elections. Surely this is the very point of having democratic elections.

As well, though the ballot envelopes were mailed out to a Kingsgrove Post Office, box number they are actually kept on the premises at the City Tattersalls Club.

Opening the outer ballot envelopes.

On the day of the counting, all the outer envelopes were opened before the scrutineers arrived at 10 am. They were presented with the inner envelope showing the name and address of the member.

Because the outer envelopes were opened before the ballot, a window of opportunity (consisting of hours, or even days?) was given for those 'unknowns' at City Tatts to see who was voting for whom. Being a comparatively small Club, it is obvious in so many cases, who would vote for who.

Did this indeed happen? Were the ballot envelopes tampered with, who knows?

Only any possible perpetrators and conspirators would know, if anything did actually occur. However, with a 48 storey building and the vast millions involved, the money motive is surely there to protect Tweedledum and Tweedledee's personal interests at any cost. Was the swapping a 1000 prepared inner envelopes, with selected votes to guarantee that the incumbent Committee is re-elected, at all possible?

THE DESTRUCTION OF CITY TATTERSALLS

Whether this, may or may not have happened, is not the point.

The essential point is, that if the ballot was held at the neutral venue, the NSW Government Electoral Office, where they once used to be conducted, there could be no possible hint of malpractice and deceit. Thereby preventing 'branch stacking' and with everyone's honour with the smell like roses. Instead, we have the present un-ethical, immoral and possibly dishonest process. The process present stinks.

Of course the amount of 1,000 is imaginary, although from the resulting count of the ballot, all the incumbent Members were re-elected with a neat 1000 extra votes separating each of them from those who stood against them. Contrary to what others may say though, I personally, believe that this separation of a neat grand of votes was just an amazing coincidence.

Now, if the election is run fairly, what I fail to understand is why Tweedledum and Tweedledee refused to act on the petition of Tatt's Members to have the election ballot off the City Tatts premises to be run by the NSW Electoral Commission. Wouldn't this would assuredly demonstrate to all those sceptics that the Club's elections, even though they are held on the premises, and the outer envelopes opened before the scrutineers arrive, are nonetheless as fair as fair can be.

In reality, the Annual Club's elections of Chairman and Committee is a sordid joke as regards any semblance of ethics and fairness - except that no one's laughing - possibly apart from Tweedledum and Tweedledee and the re-elected Committee Members.

City Tattersalls Club Rules are actually quite specific about how the elections are to be conducted:

(Ballots - how conducted)

Rule 6.15   Where a ballot is required under these Rules in relation to an office of Committee Member:

(a)   the Secretary must cause to be printed a ballot paper showing separately and in alphabetical order, the surname and also the Christian or first names (and such other description as may be made necessary by a similarity of names) of all candidates validly nominated for each office in respect of which an election is necessary;

(b)   for each Annual Election by postal vote, the ballot paper referred to in paragraph (a) must:

　　(i)   include an asterisk or similar marking adjacent to the name of each current
Committee member who is a candidate for election, and a note to the effect that the person is a current member of the Committee,"

　　(ii)   include a note to the effect that the candidates are listed in alphabetical order in accordance with the Rule's of the Club; and

　　iii)   be accompanied by a Voter Declaration;
the Returning Officer is responsible for receiving completed ballot papers and Voter Declarations, and must ensure ballot papers received by the Returning Officer are kept safe and secret...

There arises an obvious question:

Just where are the ballot papers being "kept safe and kept secret" on the Club premises at City Tattersalls Club? And by whom?

Awakening the Dead

I had a conversation with a long standing Member. It went something like this after he commented, "You know, clubs use the names and addresses of dead members to cast votes in a particular way, for apart from the Club's management who knows the names and addresses of dead members. It's a near foolproof system for without knowing the names of those Members who have died, how can any one check? "

I replied, "Are you joking, who would stoop so low?"

"Listen mate, " he said, "With big bucks involved, everything is fair game."

I couldn't argue with his logic. Corrupt organisations and political parties, do use the votes of the dead members, It's called 'Ghost Stacking'. It's one of the many aspects within the overall practice normally referred to as 'Branch Stacking'.

"However," he went on to say, "Regards the CEO and the Chairman, I am absolutely positive they would have done the decent thing by using only those dead Life Member's that they knew for certain would have voted for them, had they still been alive."

Anyway, my savant friend commented, finally "I know the Chairman wouldn't be involved, because he's a solicitor. Didn't he take the Hypnocratic Oath to uphold the Law?"

A pertinent question for the Members of City Tatts.

Do you honestly think that the Chairman of the present Committee would have been re-elected as Chairman, if he had announced honestly and bluntly that in February of 2013 the Committee resolved to mortgage the entire Club's assets including freehold for $17,540,000. Despite Rule 6 stating that the maximum amount that can be borrowed is $5,500,000 mortgage after a special meeting is convened for the Members consideration (permission)!

I think not.

This Chairman, Tweedledee, who is such an expert on the Club's Rules at the Annual General Meeting, yet blithely breaks, probably the most important Club Rule for his own purposes or agenda. He personally signed the mortgage contract '... as per the Act of 1912', but the Act, Rule 6, states he can only borrow up to $5,500.000 with the Members consent which he plainly neither sought nor obtained.

When I personally advised the Chairman and the CEO and others, that I was writing this book, Tony Guilfoyle asked, "Why?"
"Due the continual secrecy and deception." was my reply.
I don't believe the Chairman or most of the present Committee would have been elected, if their un-authorised and sleight of hand actions had been known by the Members prior to the Annual Elections in May 2013.
As well, had the annual elections should conducted fairly and squarely by the Electoral Commission, as they once used to be, this would have given a fair chance for other concerned and responsible members to be elected as Chairman and on the Committee.
Unless the present balloting system is changed, the CEO, Chairman and Committee, will do all they can to prevent the Annual Elections being conducted by the Electoral Commission to prevent any possible demolition of their 'House of Cards'.

With all the rumours, insinuations and accusations, as well as articles by the Press concerning the goings-on at City Tattersalls, surely a NSW Parliamentary Inquiry is in order before millions are spent on a proposed high rise complex, to ensure that the Club Executive and Committee act in a responsible and ethical manner for all concerned.
Altogether, the NSW public have had a gut-full with the level of corruption at all levels of Church, Politics and Club.

THE DESTRUCTION OF CITY TATTERSALLS

This book is a plea for the NSW Parliament to direct City Tattersalls to at least, have their Club Elections conducted impartially by the Electoral Commission of NSW so that the cycle of recycling the same Committee Members year after year can end, allowing others to take their place.

Also a some resignations of a few Committee Members could save them from possible future embarrassment especially if there is a Parliamentary Inquiry into the Club when Committee Members are each hauled before it to give evidence.

As the Electoral Commission of NSW was put in place to ensure and guarantee fair and impartial elections at a reasonable cost. Consequently, the question arises why would a once elite Club such as the City Tattersalls Club organise their own in-house elections at far greater cost to the Club unless there are hidden agendas together with ulterior motives for personal gain?

One can only conjecture, but I would be prepared to take a bet that they are for the the very same reasons why the same mob of Committee Members are re-elected each year.

By Tweedledum And Tweedledee

CITY TATTERSALLS CLUB

13 May 2013

Mr John Bineham
PO Box 492
STRAWBERRY HILLS POST OFFICE   NSW   2012

Dear Mr Bineham

I refer to your letter dated 1 April 2013.

I have obtained the reassurance from the Returning Officer that the usual procedure will apply. The outer envelopes will be opened by the Returning Office without the scrutineers present, but the inner envelopes (containing the ballot papers) will not be opened until 10:00am on Thursday 23 May 2013. Provided the scrutineers are there at 10:00am, no inner envelopes will be opened in their absence.

Yours faithfully

Patrick Campion
Chairman

Ode to Tweedledum and Tweedledee

Cast of Characters

Tweedledum: the CEO who is never wrong.
Tweedledee: the Chairman who is always right.
The Fools: are concerned members who try to right the Club's wrongs.
The Mushrooms: are ordinary members, kept in the dark, fed on baloney.
The Idiot: who wrote this doggerel.

Once upon a time, there was a thriving happy Club,
People thronged amidst much gaiety, lots of hub hub.
Built smack right in the middle of Sydney city,
It was in the best location that a business to be.
Each week 200,000 walked past its doors
If you truly counted, there would be many more.
But Tweedledum insists the location is quite poor
For not enough customers pass through his doors.
Well they did once, because when I joined the Club
There were 47,000 members enjoying the hub hub.
Yes replies Tweedledum I remember it well

*For when I took over, everything was swell.
Now I might be an Idiot, but it seems to me
That the Club was the best one in the whole of Sydney.
Then Tweedledum was handed a goose laying golden eggs
But he slowly killed it, until it was stone dead.
Now that's not quite true, says Tweedledum
From our $22 million profit, losses are a mere humdrum.
I run at a loss, 'cause it's part of my Strategic Business plan
Don't ask me, for I won't answer you, although I surely can.*

*Not successful, though many people past the place go
Because within, it has many delights, but nobody knows.
Now dancing is popular every few nights
Dance lessons also, just to get the steps right.
There are lots of billiard tables for snooker games
The world most famous players, once, in they came.
There's gyms and saunas, swimming pools too,
There's the restaurants and bistro, bars not a few.
There's Indoor bowls, Toastmasters, Bridge and Majong
Or go for a run with the runners, along to Bennelong.
Yet all one can see as one passes by the door
Are pokies and pokies and pokies, and nothing more.*

*Why is this so? It is not very hard to tell, so I can,
It's all part of the Club's Business Strategic Plan.
Because of the Plan, the Club purchased 194 Pitt
But its high cost knocked the Club, butt over tit.
Now it sits there quite empty, so sad and forlorn
The building's eight floors, built only to be torn down.
Dum deceived members, we were told, "Its a good deal."
But at the $9 million paid, it sure was no steal.
The interest paid on 194, is $800,000 every year,
To pay for Tweedledum's plan of a high-rise in the air.*

It's not for nothing he's called Tweedledum
There's no argument from me, says Tweedledee.
Now I'm the Chairman of City Tatts, a jolly fine solicitor
Who knows law's not a saint – she's really a whore.
I too have seen Tatts go up far, only to go down
From being the fair Queen of the Clubs,
To become the the sad Joker of Sydney town.
And although it's had lots of help from me,
It's mainly Tweededum's fault, not me Tweedledee.

Tatts is run by the Committee, who meet almost every week,
But like those three wise monkeys they can't see, hear or speak.
They are sworn to secrecy by Tweedledee
To becoming faceless men, so Members can't see.
The Members are regarded as mushrooms, so just for a lark
We'll feed them all bullshit, and keep them in the dark
What they will get from us, is the glossy quarterly magazine
Containing the greatest load of codswallop that ever been.

The elections held in 2013, the year of our Lord
Which saw all the old Committee all get back on board.
But this wouldn't have happened, if the Members had known
That the entire Club had been mortgaged, right up to the bone.
From one bank to another for an almighty fee
Well that's what $17,500,000, seems like to me.
True Tweedledee truthfully told of it in the Club's magazine
Called it a 'charge', but left the amount and mortgage unseen.
Merely a slight oversight, a typographical error,
But Tweedledee knows that if the members knew
There's no way his Chairmanship, he could renew.

For City Tattersalls is a great Club with a fine long history,
With previous members, telling tales about her, him and he.

Never before was it all mortgaged, right up to the hilt,
Because it paid its own way, ever since it was built.
I remember once, Tweedledum touted a name change
From City Tattersalls to Silks, now that's a wide range.
Instead of the odd 50, he was confronted by 500
Very angry members, who were told 'Tatts' was dead,
For he decided that 'Silks', was a much nicer name, instead.
No way! They screamed and chanted very loudly
So Tweedledum though he relented, he took it quite badly.

So if an 500 members were angered over a name change for Tatts
Then Tweedledee expect a riot, when you put to the meeting that,
The Members permission wasn't sought, to not be unkind,
For Mushrooms don't know, too much bullshit makes them blind.
But City Tattersalls Rule 6 states in no uncertain way
To mortgage the Club needs a special meeting underway,
To seek the Members permission; to let them have their say,
But the Committee voted affirmative, in an underhand way.
Then kept it secret from Members, so Tweedledum held his sway.

Now I don't mean Tweedledee, but I do accuse Tweedledum
Of keeping the Committee like puppets up on a string, strung,
Who are wheedled, conned and coerced in every what way,
By Tweedledum, who's only interested, in what he has to say.
So, to please Tweedledum, the Committee, including Tweedledee
Met for a meeting, that greatly affected the Club, you and me,
They bypassed Rule 6, of the City Tattersalls Act of 1912
To bypass the Members wrath, and their negative resolve.

So, to be, or not to be, is the City Tattersalls a legal mortgagor?
Now, Tweedledee as a lawyer, he knows well, what the law's for.
He knows, more than most of us, should it be an illegal loan,
Then from his Chairman's position, he would tumble down.

If the members had known he traded the Clubs sovereignty,
Because, to be the boss of Tattersalls, is where he wants to be.
However, if Members had known the illegal mortgage's amount
Few would've voted for him, he would have gone for the count.

This doggerel ditty was written for members to awake
To disclose the dastardly plan for all of those on the make.
Those architects, planners and developers and more,
Who will profit by asking millions by the damn score.
But let's give a big hand, for Tweedledum and Tweedledee
Without whose mighty valiant efforts, nothing could be.
But we members won't miss out, as you will plainly see
No Sir - not Joe, Jack and Jill, not you and not me.
After years of jackhammers, with the noise and dust,
Also a big gaping hole in the ground, as a necessary must.
At the eventual end, like a phoenix we will all see
Rise up a multi-storey building, but not for you or for me.

No, sadly the Club will finally become a minnow of sorts,
Concreted on all sides, built higher than anyone thought.
We will have become, an era that's long gone, a sad memory,
A once great Club, now just a paragraph of Sydney's history.
All planned by that master of spin, dearest Tweedledum
With his twin conspirator, who is of course our Tweedledee.
Some members think the Club's for those of the Who's Who,
Those fools who enjoy wining, dining, dancing, and billiards too,
But you'll rarely see in there, any member of the Committee
Because they are too busy planning for us, for you and for me.

What is the point of a Club of four stories high, no more,
Compared to a concrete building rising up so many floors.
Why Tweedledum, you have a suite on the very top floor
Yes Tweedledee, but notice, your's is right next door.

But I didn't want any reward on the top most floor
I did it, for love of the Club – no money – I'm no whore.
And yet, what can one do, when it's forced on you,
For a refusal would hurt, be the work of a cad
For I was only being clever – not really being bad.
It's just a developer repaying Tweedledum and Tweedledee
"For it couldn't have happened without them," said a grateful he.

But please never forget our ultra-sycophantic Club Committee.
Who have been as loyal and honest as anyone could ever be.
In our suites upstairs, they will always be welcomed anew
With a cup of tea, a biscuit, while enjoying our fine view.
Of course, this is doggerel is just a fairytale, everyone can tell,
Consequently, any relationship to people is purely coincidental.
What do you mean – there really is a City Tattersalls?
Gosh, I thought this amusing tale was purely accidental.
And within, are there really Tweedledum and Tweedledee?
Are they really so alike those two – Beelzebub and Mephistophles?

Johny Bineham

Chapter 5

The Proposed High Rise 48 Storey Building

Time is precious, but truth is more precious than time.
Benjamin Disraeli

Scoop! Scoop!
Remember Folks, you read it here first!!!

Public Announcement
The CEO, Tony Guilfoyle and the Chairman Patrick Campion, of City Tattersalls Club, has to an announce with much sadness, that due to OH&S concerns about the noise, dust and possible danger, from the demolition, excavation and construction being carried out in the erection of the ABSOLUTELY MAGNIFICENT high rise complex, City Tattersalls Club has no choice but to cease trade until construction is complete.
Oh dear, what has happened is a complete surprise to us in management who are left with no choice but to put off the entire staff of City Tatts until further notice.
All staff will, of course, be given first choice for their previous positions when the Club reopens in two or three years time.

Drop - drop - drop - drop - drop - these are the sounds of

the tears that have fallen on the computer and stained the paper coming from the printer, from your deeply saddened and heartfelt affected, and soon to be your former boss, Tony Guilfoyle. As well, there are a few added tears from those who were elected to look after your interests - the Members of the City Tattersalls Committee.

The high rise

There is no denying that on paper the proposed building looks quite distinct and unique. It is certainly a clever piece of modern architecture. Within the complex, City Tattersalls is assured of a new 100 seat restaurant, as well as hotel rooms and accommodation. The high rise it is hoped will give City Tattersalls other potential sources of income.

I think the architects should be congratulated on creating a fine edifice with the restrictions imposed on them by having to build alongside then up and over the existing heritage building of City Tattersalls Club.

However, usually for a gain in life there is often a loss to balance it out. The reality of the high rise is this example. A good friend of mine had a brand new high rise erected alongside the offices of his building. For three years as they dug down and built up, there was the incessant noise from building equipment, mainly jackhammers. The constant noise was absolutely incessant.

Now I cannot imagine people gambling, playing billiards or card games, or dancing in such a noisy and dusty area. Even though the CEO and the Chairman have assured me and others personally that the Club will trade normally during building construction. Well, where I might once have believed them, I certainly don't anymore.

In real terms, even if the Club is kept open, do you really believe that the gambling (for revenue), the restaurants, the sub-Club activities will continue as normal with a vast high rise complex being erected over the two or three years construction?

No, I believe the Club will have little choice but to close its doors, not just because of the noise and possible danger listed by OH&S, but more importantly, because they will be trying their utmost to complete the building and fit it out in the quickest possible time. People will just hamper and slow down this process, and, 'time is money' don't we all know.

Quite apart from that, have you ever seen or heard of a business being conducted while there is a huge construction site on, and around, and on top of that premises?

No you haven't, funny that - neither have I. The idea that City Tattersalls will continue to trade is pure propaganda put our to convince you to vote for the high rise.

I have been informed that the club will be able to continue trading because there will be a high, wide and handsome wall erected between the club and the construction site. It might as well be a wall of money because of the cost associated with the erection of such an edifice.

However, my satirical side has kicked in to say that irrespective whether it costs 2, 5 or $10 million, I believe that rather than being a wall, it is a actually a smokescreen to hide the real truth, in order to suck Members into voting for the high rise.

Once the Members vote for the construction, with contracts signed, one reason or another will be found, most likely cost and impracticality, to not erect the wall as it would be cheaper and safer to close down the Club for the duration of the construction. Alas, only time will tell if my supposition is correct or not.

Strata Levels
Warning! Beware! Take note!

THE DESTRUCTION OF CITY TATTERSALLS

City Tattersalls Club pays no rent, BUT this will no be the case if Tweedledum negotiates for extra levels that are 'strata titles'.

The strata fees, which are forever, could put City Tattersall in a rental situation that is highly detrimental to the Club by placing a financial noose around the Club's neck that could see it swinging high from a financial gibbet that would slowly but surely choke the life out of the Club.

At present the Club pays no rent, so why would one want to put the Club into an unnecessary rental situation when Tweedledum can't make a profit even with rent free premises, so what hope would he have if the Club paid rent?

I and other Members suggest the Members to think hard and long about the future of the Club. The high rise and its plans won't disappear if the high rise is postponed into the future when the Club is run properly by a different Executive and Committee. There are those amongst the present mob who seem to be hell bent on the destruction of the Club, either through blissful ignorance or are they also are in cahoots with the Machiavellian machinations of 'the few'.

A little hard thinking now along with some common sense can save a lot of tears at a later date.

The human cost

So assembling the picture in human terms - what is the cost if the high rise goes ahead for the staff?

Well there is the distinct possibility of a huge human cost and loss associated with this high rise project. The CEO, the Chairman and the Committee are putting their dream, their personal agenda for the future of the Club, up against nearly all the staff becoming 'collateral damage', which is just a nice American euphemism for being 'killed off'; thrown on the scrap heap, as a necessary part of the costs.

By Tweedledum And Tweedledee

Tweedledum and Tweedledee of course, might put it this way, "That's life and you can't stop progress." So it's quite probable that it's onwards and upwards for 48 storeys, but at what human cost to the Club?

Actually with little to no trade, the staff will become redundant and have to go. This doesn't include, of course, Tony and his mob who might be left with little choice but to take that 'unintended' but 'extended' holiday on full pay.

Please do correct me if I am wrong, but I believe that virtually all the staff will lose their jobs if the high rise goes ahead. However it will be an even sadder fate for all of those who had the misfortune to have their Super in the Tatts Fund, for they won't have any Super money to fall back on to when they are permanently dismissed, or put off for the duration of the construction.

So, as I put my crystal ball back into its box, that's about sums up for me the future situation for City Tattersalls if the high rise goes ahead as presently proposed. To my Member friends, as well as my friends among the staff at City Tattersalls, I actually do hope I'm wrong.

Looking after your's truly.
What I do believe is that the CEO, Tweedledum has taken out for himself and a few of his executive a contract that will allow him and his cronies will have their salaries continue while the building is in progress - why?

Well it's only being sensible, isn't it. Too bad, too sad, for all the rest of the staff who aren't in his small clique. It's out into the cold, cold snow of being jobless for them, all for the good of a few. For the 'future' of the Club, the many will be sacrificed. I hope and pray I'm wrong, but taking a reality check, I believe the entire club will become a building site for the time it takes to build and fit out the 50 storey structure..

THE DESTRUCTION OF CITY TATTERSALLS

Even though I can only conjecture, yet I firmly believe those extraordinary costs such as salaries during construction, are the real reasons why the Club was mortgaged for $17,540,000. It was to pay for all the added costs, and there are many when putting up a huge high rise; agent's fees, architects fees, lawyers fees, consultants fees, potential loss of salaries, etc etc. The $17,540,000 wasn't for upgrading the gambling, which was the Chairman Tweedledee's reason for the loan, as he stated in the Club magasine. In reality, it was to offset all the associated costs accrued during the time it takes to build a high rise.

Again, I haven't have the slightest amount of animosity towards the CEO and the Chairman, for when it is all said and done people continue to act in accordance with their natures. I seriously wish Tony and Patrick, lives full of health, wealth and success, just so long as they both stay well away from City Tattersalls Club. One purpose for this book is to assist towards that very end, because as far as their track record with City Tattersalls is concerned they have been unmitigated disasters.

What's worse, is that the 'destruction' of City Tattersalls has been deliberate and purposeful in order to run it down financially so that there is no recourse but to sell the high rise to 'save' the Club.

This becomes absolutely ludicrous when there is 200,000 passing trade per week, year after year surging past the Club. Yet there is not even one teeny weeny sign advertising all the social activities going on in the Club. inviting visitors to participate in the Club's activities and amenities.

The Club should be packing them in, both gamblers and revelers, while making a fortune. But no, even the Club's web site has not until now ever mentioned, let alone promote the activities of the sub-Clubs, not even promote the successful

By Tweedledum And Tweedledee

Dinner Dances. It's as though they did not exist, when they are at the very heart of the Club, the primary reason for the Club's existence. But daily, weekly, monthly and yearly, it is gambling, gambling and more gambling.

Even the dumbest of dimwits, even a moron running, would surely advise the public of the Club's social activities within the Club to attract business, but apparently neither the Tatts CEO, Chairman or Committee see the commercial return in doing so. All of this commercial mismanagement only makes sense when you realise the Club has been purposely run down for the personal agenda and future gains for the 'few'.

And, and it is a big AND, should the high rise happen, these self-same two, Tweedledee and Tweedledum, would still be involved in the running one way or the other of the complex (most likely lucrative management contracts) for their very own purposes and to suit their very own agendas. Of course, any such any such contract would still be negotiated and conducted in secrecy and deceit. Simply because it very hard for anyone to change their nature and the manner of the ways that they conduct their lives.

The following story will illustrate my point:

A scorpion wanted to cross a flooded stream. So it pleaded with a frog to ferry it across the stream on its back. The frog said, "Why should I do that, you will sting and kill me."

The scorpion replied, "That would be crazy, because then we would both drown."

The frog seeing the logic of this statement agreed to carry the scorpion across the stream. But half way across, the scorpion suddenly stung the frog.

The mortally wounded and dying frog exclaimed in horror, "Why did you do this - we will both surely die!"

"Ah, I'm really sorry - but it's my nature."

THE DESTRUCTION OF CITY TATTERSALLS

Superannuation
I won't say much about the City Tattersalls Superannuation disaster for its subscribers but I will portray the financial disaster in human terms by telling one person's story. He worked at Tatts for some 30 years during which time he accumulated around $420,000 in super funds. A reasonable nest egg for his retirement. He has used up $170,000 over the years, which left $8,000 remaining in his super account.

No - my maths are OK, what I am saying is that $8,000 is all that is left, for $242,000 of his funds just disappeared.

As of early 2014, his remaining $250,000 has diminished to around $8000, and even that piddling remaining amount is now frozen. Well, it can't get any worse you say.

Yes it can - it gets much worse, for City Tattersalls Superannuation Fund is in receivership. So have a guess how much in the dollar he will finally receive (.50 or .25c??), and when?

You may not be aware that City Tattersalls Super was once the second best performing Super Fund in NSW with accumulated funds of around many millions until it was pillaged by a couple of smart operators.

So much for the past, but who is currently in charge and being paid to run the Super Fund - go on - guess?

You're right - of course, it's Tweedledum, our CEO Tony, who is ably assisted by his mate, Mark Cooper. Oh, what was that noise I just heard?

Was that a sigh of relief, now that the Super is in the hands of two financial whiz kids?

Unnecessary angst.
I had to pick up some tickets for the Dinner Dance. Once it was so simple, "Four tickets please." I pays me money and am handed 4 tickets from the ticket machine. I check the floor

plan for table I want - all done. I am out of the Club in five, make that six minutes flat.

Now (in March of 2014), it's a wait for ten minutes for an antiquated computer system to warm up. Fill in the necessary information, another ten minutes, then a final wait for a printout, all up - about thirty five minutes. So while waiting, and waiting, I had plenty of time to look around. Was there in the foyer or elsewhere any signs anywhere to let patrons know what was actually happening in the Club that day? Or that week? Or that month?

No, no, no. Surely if you want people to attend functions, fill restaurants, billiards rooms, dance floors surely the most basic of marketing strategies is to let people know what's going on - but not at City Tattersalls.

But then I've told you why. The Club is not marketed for local, interstate or overseas visitors that walk by daily in droves, just so the management can consistently run the Club down and into bank debt so massive that they have no recourse left but to sell the high rise to save the Club - for the Members - for the staff?

Of course not. The high rise has always been planned for a small clique who are out to benefit themselves

Is there an alternative?

Of course, scrap or delay the high rise. Market City Tattersalls Club properly by getting a decent CEO. One who can actually run the Club and rid ourselves of this dunderhead Tweedledum who can manipulate everything except make a profit with Tatts, when it is surrounded in an ocean of money, just waiting to be tapped into with the most basic of marketing skills.

Speedily, eliminate the 'unnecessary manufactured debt' by having Tatts make money from the sea of customers that haven't a clue about Tatts amenities and services.

Turn the place once again into the rip roaring crowd pleaser that it used to be with services and amenities that the Member want, together with food and drinks at prices that attract.

Elect a people's Chairman who can interact with the Members and run both the Club and the CEO with an iron fist.

Get a CEO that isn't a recluse, locked away in his office, with his secretary Jan Elks constantly standing (or sitting) on guard. Mind you, she's is great (for Tony's privacy), the last time I rang about a pre-arranged meeting, I was told by Jan, "It will be three weeks."

"What three weeks before I can see him?" asks I.

"No, it will be three weeks before you can phone him." Bloody hell, it's easier organising a meeting with the Premier.

Of course - he's a very private person you know - try and find a photo of him anywhere. Google 'images' for Tony Guilfoyle, and notice that the CEO of one of the major Clubs in Australia is nowhere to be seen. What's more, that's how he wants it, so he can always slip under the radar undetected - not a photo anywhere.

Some medico explained to me that Tweedledum most probably has a condition known medically as *Scopophobia*, which is a morbid fear of being seen, or being photographed. Quite sad really, but not much good when one is running a social club, a people's place.

Of course, if you have been 'naughty' and have to do a 'runner' from the country, it's nice to know there isn't a photograph anywhere that could be used by Interpol to trace you.

Certainly, for any lasting change, new Committee Members need to be elected who have the guts to say to the CEO, 'No - enough is enough - now you start running the Club our way. Start making piles of money' and when we say jump Tony, all we want to hear from you is - "How high?"

Fill the place by day and by night. Fill the restaurants, the dance floors, the bars and bistro, instead of doing your level best to empty them so the high rise can be sold to save it.

The very first thing is a sign highly visible at the front entrance:
Welcome to all interstate and overseas visitors'
Why not make City Tattersalls Club your own personal Club for the duration of your stay in Sydney.
Come in and enjoy our range of wining, dining, dancing, our gyms, our billiards, Toastmasters.
Come in to share in our friendly atmosphere.

"By jingo, we couldn't do that," says Tweedledum, "Invite strangers in to enjoy our facilities. If we start filling the restaurants we will have to employ more staff. If we fill the dance floors we may have to have more nights of dancing with people noisily enjoying themselves with Ballroom and Salsa, when they should be downstairs quietly playing the pokies."

"Just imagine if overseas people from the international hotels conveniently located just around the corner and up the street, actually came in to play our pokies, now it would hardly be fair to take money away from the Casino, would it?"

Anyway, says Tweedledum, it far easier to borrow money from the bank. When we mortgaged the entire City Tattersalls Club including the freehold, it wasn't so difficult. It wasn't as though I've had to personally mortgage my own property.

The NSW Parliament act to ensure lasting change.

Surely the NSW Parliament has the power to insist and ensure that the Club elections be run by the Electoral Commission of NSW. Then, should the present Chairman and Committee be elected fairly and squarely I will personally congratulate all of them on their success at being elected, as well, pull my head in.

Until proper elections are held at City Tattersalls, I will continue to belittle, berate and satirise, which will make them, Tweedledum and Tweedledee, famous, but for all the wrong reasons (now how many people have books written about them?). In the battle to return City Tatter salls Club back into the hands of fairly elected Committee members and rid the Club of Tony Guilfoyle, this is merely the opening salvo of as many broadsides as it takes.

I, and others, will continue until the City Tattersalls is run as it used to be, ethically and profitably for the benefit of the Members - not merely for the whim and at the whimsy, of the CEO and Chairman.

If any of the Club or Committee have the idiocy to delegate Tweedledum, a comparative miniscule sardine in the rough and tumble of the Sydney business world in any capacity to negotiate for the Club with the professional great white sharks of the NSW building industry, then we are already DOOMED.

With their experience, from the very beginning they will have easily recognized you as the type who is so puffed up with self-manufactured hubris that even a modicum of flattery about your own imagined extraordinary brilliance will have you eating out of their back-handers.

Chapter 6

"...none of us really changes over time; we only become more fully what we are."
Lestat in Anne Rice's *Queen of the Damned*

A Vision of a Future for City Tattersalls.

In order to finish with the past and prepare for a bright and shining future, the first, the foremost and the most essential step, is to get rid of the CEO, Tony Guilfoyle, the Chairman Patrick Campion, as well as those deadwood on the Committee who supported the un-authorised massive bank loan for $17,540,000..

We need a new Chairman and Committee - why?

Because instead of the elected Chairman and Committee instructing the CEO (Secretary) by issuing orders and directions on how they want the Club to operate, in effect the 'dog rightly wagging its tail'.

Unfortunately, the opposite actually occurs with the CEO directing the Chairman and Committee on how he wants the Club run, literally the 'tail wagging the dog'.

Make no mistake, the Club's Rules are quite specific on this matter:
29.   Secretary
29.1   There must be only one Secretary of the Club. The

By Tweedledum And Tweedledee

Secretary is to be appointed by the Committee at remuneration and on conditions determined by the Committee and shall hold office during the Committee's pleasure or for such period as it may appoint. The Secretary is also deemed to be the General Manager and the Chief Executive Officer of the Club for the purposes of the Act.

29.2 Any appointment of a Secretary by the Committee must be subject to approval by the Licensing Court under the Act.

29.3 The Secretary shall, on all occasions in the execution of his office: act under the superintendence and control of the Committee; and be responsible to the Committee.

The instructions of the Committee are sufficient authority for any of the Secretary's acts.

It states clearly and unequivocally above in rule 29.3:
The Secretary shall, on all occasions in the execution of his office: act under the superintendence and control of the Committee; and be responsible to the Committee.

No where do the Club Rules state that the Secretary, the CEO shall run the Club without being directed by the Chairman or the Committee.

It has become patently obvious for the Club's future survival and growth that a bright new confident, ethical Chairman, together with new Committee Members are needed to once again gain control of the Club if City Tattersalls is to restore its high standing as a social Club that's run for the benefit of its Members.

City Tattersalls Club needs for the people of Sydney to rise high again like a Golden Phoenix instead of sink like the Dead Duck it has become. Even the finest ship with the best crew must eventually flounder with an incompetent captain and first mate at the helm.

However, with competent management, the commercial and social success of City Tatts is assured purely because of its amazing and brilliantly placed commercial position.

With the right management and committee, Tatts would again become the centrepiece, 'the' meeting place, for the best inter-mingling and socialising with the best of Sydney Town.

Unfortunately, we, the concerned Members of the Club, are stuck in a ludicrous position because we're not in a position to rid ourselves of an incompetent CEO, because that is the job of the elected Committee who haven't either the brains, guts, or the brawn, to do their job and remove him.

Even worse - we Members can't elect a new Committee because of the elections are run in-house and on the Club's premises, and by a questionable and highly expensive Returning Officer, instead of being held impartially at far lower costs in the neutral premises of the NSW Electoral Office. The present flawed process ensures the annual re-election of the same Chairman and Committee.

City Tattersalls has both the position and the space, especially on the second floor, to create a multifunctional venue that can house a wide range of activities, including exhibitions for art, photography and cultural events.

It would also allow that dancing in all its forms of social interaction, including large balls when the occasions arise. I know, the Town Hall venue as priced itself out of the market for International Dance competitions where you may have up to 1000 in attendance. Just imagine so many people needing refreshments over an entire weekend with City Tattersalls catering for such a large group.

The Powerhouse Arts Centre at Casula, drew in crowds of

By Tweedledum And Tweedledee

20,000 and 30,000, at exhibitions on the Korean and Vietnam wars. I know this, because I was the Curator of the Korean War exhibition, titled *The Vagrant Winds*.

If this can successfully occur in an out of the way place in the outer suburbs, imagine, what the potential would be for a similar exhibition located in the very heart of the CBD.

City Tattersalls has a capacity to be and should be, the cultural and social hub in the heart of Sydney, for it is in the unique position of being very close to the two main underground railway stations in the Sydney CBD. City Tattersalls has no need to entice people into the city, the people (millions of them) are already here living and working in the CBD. Many, many more business people and city staff, should be using City Tattersalls as their Club for social interaction as they did in previous years.

Below is an excerpt from a previous publication of City Tattersalls to illustrate that City Tattersalls had an unique and prestigious place in Sydney society.

The following description was taken from the Club's Annual Report of 1927:
"The Second Annual Ball, this year in aid of the funds of the Children's Hospital, was held in the Palais Royal, Moore Park, on Thursday July 19th, in the presence of his Excellency the Governor, Sir Dudley de Chair, and Lady de Chair.

The Governor, accompanied by Major Longfield Lloyd, arrived at 9.15 and later on, after the Zimbalist concert, Lady de Chair and Miss Elaine de Chair arrived. They were accompanied by Brig.-General and Mrs. H.W.Lloyd and Mrs Longfield Lloyd. A unique bouquet, composed of sweets and covered with blue and gold tin foil, bearing the Club's colours, was presented to Lady de Chair by Mrs J.Clarke, wife of the Chairman, on behalf of the Ladies' Committee, and "Miss

THE DESTRUCTION OF CITY TATTERSALLS

Australia 1927" (Miss Phylis Von Alwyn) was the recipient of a handsome tortoiseshell toilet cabinet from the Members of the Club, as a token of her success.

That the function eclipsed all anticipations, both financially and otherwise, can be taken from the following headlines of newspaper reports on the function: 'The Season s Gayest', 'Originality at City Tatt's Club Charity Ball', 'Nothing Short of a Triumph'.

Headlines are from three of our leading dailies.

So City Tatttersalls was an once integral part of Sydney society taking an active part in the life-flow of the city. But to have a spirited Club you need spirited men to run it.

Sadly, under the auspices of our present deadwood management where social interaction and Member participation have become dirty words,

City Tattersalls simply refuses to market itself to the millions arriving in the city to work let alone the half a million people living and renting in the inner-city and close environs, most of whom had never been inside of City Tattersalls. Let alone, be aware of all the facilities such as male and female gyms, swimming pools, as well as, the many sub-Clubs such as Billiards, Gourmet Tastings, Toastmasters, runners, dancers, Bridge, Ma Jong, etc.

Being in such a prime business location, City Tattersalls should be running or organizing the running of leadership courses, or other activities that attract a range of people and therefore potential members into the club.

Surely, even considering the present level of incompetency, the present management and Committee could somehow manage to think a little outside the square of poker machines and gambling. Surely Tatts is more than just a pokie-palace.

By Tweedledum And Tweedledee

My vision for City Tattersalls Club.
My vision for City Tattersalls is a Club of the Members, for the Members, which was its original vision, aim and aspiration for its future, by its farsighted Founding Fathers.

Please read what Reg Culhane, who served in the Great War, had to say about his ideas for City Tattersalls, "My reason for wanting to serve on the Committee was simple. I believed that if we gave more amenities to Members they would stay longer and the Club would prosper."

I am in total agreement with Reg Culhane. Tweedledum has done the absolute opposite, he has eliminated more amenities than any other person to the obvious detriment of the Membership and Club. My vision would be to reverse his philosophy of destruction and increase amenities for the Members in all directions with some initial star-up costs but with the capacity for high returns in revenue and Membership.

Firstly, the entrance to City Tattersalls should be a magnificently appointed welcoming Coffee Lounge that beckons and welcomes members and visitors. This would be on the right facing the present main entrance. The gambling would still be there but out of sight to those in the Coffee Lounge. The aroma from the high quality of the coffee beans alone has been proven to be successful in attracting coffee customers.

Re-introduce that most successful, that most popular, and that most distinctive attraction which previously was the 'Jewel in the Crown' at City Tattersalls - the Buffet, the Smorgasbord. However, design it to be in tune with today's changes in Sydney's palate.

Of course have the traditional English Roast of the Day, with baked veges, the soup and the sweets, as well as a vegetarian section and salad bar. But included should be a half dozen of the most popular Thai, Chinese and Indian dishes. The buffet should be located in the Zest Restaurant area.

Introduce courses similar to Toastmasters, to develop speaking and executive social skills for the young up and coming executives of Sydney town. This is a way of grooming future executives of Sydney's businesses to join as Club Members.

Capitalise on the Club's CBD location smack in the middle of three of the finest hotels for overseas visitors by having a Cultural Centre showing off the Arts and Music of Sydney. Sunday should be the busiest day of the week. Surely this is preferable to just closing up shop for the day, which was last century's style of business.

Have the Celebrity Room constantly full of life. It's mainly unoccupied space during most days when it should hold social activities such as dance and music. In today's busy world many people don't have the time to learn to dance as exercise, pleasure and socialising until they retire. Why not have free dance classes for the over 45s in the usually empty by day Celebrity room. Anything and everything to have Members and guests come and enjoy themselves.

Most importantly, advertise the Club's activities to the surrounding millions of workers and those living permanently in the city and inner city. At present and for years past, no one either inside or outside knows for sure just what is available or going on at the Club on any given day, unless you carry around the Club's magazine in your pocket - but who does that?

"Well Pat does!"

"Which Pat?"

"Oh him!"

That little discourse was the result of a comment by Tweedledee when I complained there wasn't any notices or signage anywhere to advise Members, guests, visitors and passersby of what was happening in the Club on any given day. The Chairman exclaimed, "It's all in the Club magazine!"

City Tattersalls was renowned for the quality and variety of its cuisine. The Esperanto Room even now, must be one of the most well appointed restaurants in Sydney. Contrary to the Esperanto's architectural ambience, we have Tony's Zest Restaurant, which has four walls, tables and chairs, with little else to lend itself to the enjoyment of one's meal.

The walls for many years were completely undecorated, unadorned and lacking in any sense of charm. To rectify this situation, I suggested that City Tattersalls conduct an acquisitive Art Competitions, which would mean eventually having paintings by Australia's premier artists hanging on the walls of our restaurants.

Well-heeled people, follow top artists is a fact. So the Club displaying the works of prominent artists would not only attract more diners but would also create a pleasant sense of dining ambience, instead of the present poverty stricken atmosphere in some areas.

The last time I suggested having art and photograph competitions was at the one and only meeting of the sub-Clubs when John Kennedy first became Chairman. He stated emphatically that the sub-Clubs would meet with him twice a year. Twice a year - there hasn't been a single meeting of the sub-Clubs since!

The Objects of the Club.

The basic problem besetting City Tattersalls is one of vision and direction. Tweedledum's vision is of 'merely customers for gambling'. He once lined up a the managers of the Club and stated bluntly,"**We want customers, not Members.**" Still remember that meeting, Tony?

The Founding father's aims and objects of the Club was all about benefits for the Members. They spelt out the aims of City Tattersalls so:

4.1   (a) to provide social, sporting, athletic, cultural and other activities for its members;

(b) to provide a clubhouse or clubhouses for the entertainment and recreation of its members;

(c) to assist any charitable, social, patriotic or philanthropic object; and so on.

The 'objects' are all about benefits to Members. Contrary to this, our Tweedledum Tony became the CEO it has been all about Tony first, mates second, gambling third, Members and sub-Clubs lagging somewhere at the rear.

Let's get real, the reasons for the high rise is really about benefits to Tony and his cohorts - any benefits to Members will be offset with higher costs for everything including food and drink.

Before this CEO got his claws clutched into the Club, the food and drinks were well below standard prices, but not now. But I don't need to tell you that.

It's not rocket science, the huge profits from gambling should be going back to the Members in lower prices and more amenities, instead it's going to pay an over-sized and over-paid executive staff, as well as vast consultant fees, necessary for a CEO who can't act on his own behalf, plus trips overseas for the favoured few, etc.

The present and future wellbeing of City Tattersalls Club, means going back to the basic aims and objects of providing amenities and services to its Members not its customers.

By Tweedledum And Tweedledee

A future high rise may be a good thing but not if Tweedledum and Tweedledeee are involved. I say this based on their Club track record to date, at a performance rather than at a personal level.

2014 - A Year of Change.

2014 will be a year of change for the City Tattersalls Club for there are now moves afoot for the sale of the high-rise with a 48 storey building to be built over the Club. Whether this goes ahead is up to a vote by the Members, as it should be.

But, and it is a big BUT, the capacity for mismanagement and incompetence won't disappear with or without the high-rise. It will only disappear when the present Committee are replaced by new blood on the Committee who are prepared to rid the Club of its very bad apple, the single-handed and single-most cause of its woes and bad tidings.

There are still some who refuse to believe how rotten City Tattersalls has been managed, and say, "Oh it's not so bad, some aspects are OK."

This comment reminds me of a joke known as 'the Curate's Egg'.

This young fresh faced and 'aim to please at any price' Curate was invited to dine at the evening meal of the Vicar and his wife.

During the dinner the Vicar's wife exclaimed," Oh dear me Curate, I believe I've served you up a boiled egg that's rotten!"

"Oh Madam, parts of it are admirable." he servilely replied.

However, for most of us, a rotten egg is a rotten egg with none of it at all admirable.

Of course, nothing can, or will change, and 'well they' know it, unless the Annual Elections for Chairman and Committee are held off the premises impartially by the Electoral Commission of New South Wales.

Within this present air of anti-crime and corruption at both the State and Federal Levels, surely there is sufficient resolve and good-will from the NSW Parliament to force City Tattersalls to have their Ballot for Committee Members conducted by the Electoral Commission. Thus ensuring that the Club can elect without fear or favour those responsible for the running of a Club that is so much an iconic part of this Sydney city we love.

But even better than that, would be a Parliamentary Inquiry into the running of City Tattersalls together with an independent audit - oh happy days!

Chapter 7

City Tattersalls Dancing

"He has no enemies, but is intensely disliked by his friends."
    Oscar Wilde

This Addendum is an extra add-on for one specific reason. A few nights ago, I and Monica were going dancing at the City Tatts dance. It was actually Friday night 14 March of this year, 2014.
 As we were about to leave all dolled up for the dance when my phone rang, on it was a message from Lorraine whom we had hoped to see there. "Don't come as there is no dance. We weren't advised that there was a function on instead."

Luckily, I had a text message warning us there was no dance because of some function that no dancer was advised of. I was lucky, but what about the other 20 to 30 people who arrived at the Celebrity Room expecting to meet with friends and enjoy a dance, only to find the venue used for other purposes.
  Unfortunately for them, this would have been after paying to park their cars.
  What I find especially galling is that at no time over the ten years passed have I received an apology from management for

By Tweedledum And Tweedledee

their lack of consideration, their lack of courtesy, and their lack of common decency, in not making alternate arrangements, or at the very least advising the Dance Committee or the Dance Coordinator that the venue wasn't available. After many confrontations, occasionally management would deign to offer an alternate venue, but not last Friday night. So after years and years of time wasted, Tweedledum hasn't changed any his black spots denoting his disdain of the dancers.

The Dance Committee built the Dance Club up to over 150 Members, the largest of all the sub-Clubs. Now I may be wrong but what really irks Tony, what makes him really uneasy, is when there is a group of people in the Club that might in any way impinge upon his power base.

Well I'm certainly looking forward to the degree of impingement that this book might have cause to pierce his delicate pale hide or his super-sensitive psyche.

Some years ago when Tweedledum first became CEO, the place was packed out on Monday, Wednesday and Friday nights but especially Friday nights. Those evenings were amazing social events, for the Celebrity Room was full of people, most of whom were dancers but not all. Some merely came to enjoy the music, the ambience, or just be among a great mix of people.

For as long as I could remember, City Tattersalls dance was the place to be on a Friday night. One had to be there by 7 o'clock for any chance of a table. Even though the place was packed with revellers, I can't recall ever seeing a fight.

Of course, as an added addition there was the buffet, which had the 'wow' factor. Because when one visited the buffet for the first time, it was hard not to say "wow." It was simply the best. But of course, Tweedledum thought otherwise and the

THE DESTRUCTION OF CITY TATTERSALLS

buffet exists no more, even though he promised it would re-open when the Club's renovations were complete.

Sadly at City Tattersalls, ballroom dancing is in the doldrums simply because Tony Guilfoyle has done its level best to rid the Club of dancing and the dancers. His rationale behind this is simple and we have discussed it at length on a number of occasions, "Dancers don't drink."

Of course he's not so quick to say that now because when I ran the Dance Club, we on the Dance Committee had packed out the Dinner Dances that continue to this day, without any promotion whatsoever from the management. So successful were the Dinner Dances that we ploughed back well over $300,000 to the Club in turnover. By the way $2,000 or over, is taken at the bar for drinks on an evening.

His statement that, "Dancers don't drink." on a normal dance night, is partially true. For when the music is playing, people get up to dance and drinking any beverage is of secondary importance. However, some dancers do wine and dine, also some play the pokies before the dance as well as after the dance. It's a pity that Tweedledum could never quite grasp the bigger picture about the dance scene.

However, before Tweedledum demolished the buffet, a group of us dancers, eight in all, would spend over $80,000 during the course of the year on wining dining and dancing, Not any more though, for my friends simply had enough of arriving only to be see the Celebrity Room let out for some other function. Too late did we realise that it was all a part of Tony's plan to demolish both the buffet and the dancing.

Tony Guilfoyle stated to me on a number of occasions, "The Celebrity Room is not only for the dancers."

By Tweedledum And Tweedledee

I replied, "I know, we dancers have no problem with that, all we want is the courtesy of letting us know in advance when a function is going to be on."

As functions are booked well ahead, all we asked for was the dates of the functions in advance so we can advise the dancers.

Oh, can't do that, or won't do that! For time after time, on ten separate occasions during one two-year period, functions were held in the Celebrity Room without bothering to advise the dancers that the venue won't be available.

Of course, the dance numbers plummeted from around 150 or 135 on a Friday night, down to the 20s and 30s. No matter how I complained, no matter what I have requested, this abominable low-bred form of crass bad manners towards Members and dancers continued on unabated until this present day.

Having put up with and wasted my time on visit after visit, meeting after meeting, with assurance after assurance, that things would change, but didn't - well, let's see what effect, what response, this book will have upon improving the situation.

I am more than happy to state that some persons in management over the past years took to upon themselves to advise me of coming functions so I could advise the dancers in advance, but no sooner was this organized, when within six months that person left City Tatts for greener fields.

It had always been a private arrangement between the function lass and myself, for not once has any arrangement been put in place to advise dancers in advance of some coming function from anyone on high in management.

I've told Tony Guilfoyle in his office, to his face, that he 'couldn't run a fish and chip shop'. He laughed, even when I told him I'm not joking. So let me state again in print, "Tony, you couldn't run a fish and chip shop."

You certainly can't run City Tattersalls Club, the proof being that since you became CEO the membership has committed suicide when compared to former numbers, as well, around 50% of the previous amenities and services either have been eliminated or decimated." I feel your record sinks under the weight of its lack of merit.

Now, I can well understand how Tweedledum would have problems running the complex and high revving Club that it once used to be, but even now with the Club being run down to only a shadow of its former self, to mainly a poker machine palace with little else compared to previous times. Tweedledum continues to demonstrate that he still can't make a go of City Tattersalls as a business with his chronic annual and now traditional losses.

Tweedledum over the last ten years has caused hundreds of Members to depart the dance scene, thousands of Members to desert the place. His decade as the CEO has caused the desolation and destruction of a Club that many held dear.

With such a background of ongoing abominable failures in the management of a social Club, how could anyone of a reasonable and sane mind consider that Tweedledum could suddenly develop the necessary expertise, to be involved in any successful running, of any aspect of a 48 storey high rise complex.

ADDENDUM A

Time is precious, but truth is more precious than time.
    Anon

Some relevant internet excerpts from:
    Save City Tatts
    City Tatts Members forum
    City Tatts Information Desk

How Tony Guilfoyle was appointed as City Tatts CEO in 2003.
Most Members don't realise what a treasure we have in Tony Tweedledum. After reading his profile how could one not hire him.
The following document is one of the most extraordinary we have ever read.
We believe it was presented by John Healy and Keith Free to the Committee of City Tattersalls Club in 2003 to support the appointment of Tony Guilfoyle as CEO (the most disastrous appointment in the history of the Club). It was probably written by Guilfoyle himself with help from Michelle Abbey. We have not altered the document in any way.
There is so much that we are tempted to say but instead we simply suggest that you read it for yourself in the light of what has happened to the Club since then

The Appointment – Tony Guilfoyle to City Tattersalls Club

Silks City Tatts is in an extraordinarily fortunate position that, as a result of excellent succession planning, Tony Guilfoyle, the Assistant General Manager, is now perfectly positioned to assume the role of General Manager of the club in February 2004. .

For over 19 years Tony has been immersed within the club and has displayed a key and prominent role in ensuring the club's success in highly challenging and uncertain times, the like of which this industry and this Board has never seen before.

In considering the picture of the person/profile created for this role. the decision now becomes straightforward. In appointing any candidate, it is vital to look at those behaviours in a particular role, (which enables elimination of the subjectivity or guesswork from the decision to hire) by very carefully assessing how the tasks and situations of the job have been handled in the past and considering how the role will need to be fulfilled in the future.

The listed key points demonstrate clearly. the presence of the knowledge, skills, ability/attitudes needed to deliver the outcomes-critical to the success of the club moving forward. The following accomplishments add clarity and confirmation to this fit. They are:

• Tony Guilfoyle has been sitting on the Club Gaming Council of Australia since 1997. This Council is restricted to a body of 34 people, the majority of whom are Chief Executive Officers

• Masquerade, in the past, advised the board of Silks City Tatts of forthcoming restrictions, and as a result, the club took a position of debt of $10.7 million to expand. This doubled the

THE DESTRUCTION OF CITY TATTERSALLS

gaming machines to some 437 and allowed the club to. grow this market.

Now, three years later, the restrictions of 450 machines has allowed the club to continue to successfully and profitably grow revenue. The licenses now have value of approximately $25,000 each so this increase in the number of machines has immediately provided the club with additional assets worth approximately $5 million

• The club has successfully traded through one of the most severe major downturns over the past three years. Since Masquerade was established the results have been significantly above .the club industry average. All this has been achieved in spite of the restrictions of a three-hour shutdown, no external advertising, no direct promotions or incentives and no cheque cashing facilities. Reinforcing this achievement, all revenue figures within Silks City Tatts are up by industry and competitive comparisons.

• Earlier this month 1500 clubs in New South Wales were rated on gaming machine income. Silks City Tatts has gone against all trends into a position of number 19, its highest ever. This extraordinary result has been achieved with . increased opposition from clubs, pubs and casinos. with none of the restrictions that Silks City Tatts has encountered

• Tony Guilfoyle has clearly demonstrated the ability to manage the club and combat the legislative restrictions as well as out manoeuvre some major new competitors (EST, CBD, etc) with reliance only on foot traffic, no parking facilities (as well as suburban competition with only weekend closures of 3 hrs with none of the above mentioned restrictions) and other setbacks,

• Has generated record trading conditions in some of the toughest and most unpredictable environments. the industry and the country has seen (11t' September 2001, SARS, war in

By Tweedledum And Tweedledee

Iraq, tourism downturn, global and local fear and caution, the Bali tragedy etc) _
• Has initiated full business unity of accounts and created this increased business clarity and the appropriate accounting principles. so educated decisions can be made based on sound commercial and business practice • Led parties overseas to identify trends and patterns in the restaurant, bar and hotel markets to enable the club to identify, implement and maintain a unique marketing edge based on valid research. This has now started.to ensure members nmx obtain club facilities based on global best practice.
• Was instrumental in identifying the need for a strong marketing presence early this year to continue to ensure the Club's differentiation and branding in this highly competitive marketplace. He has now successfully appointed a superbly qualified Marketing Director based on implementing strong strategic management skills and rigorous selection processes. One of the key reasons Silks City Tatts was able to attract Michelle Abbey, from WestfieldlLend Lease to the club, was as a direct result of Tony Guilfoyle's ability to communicate the vision and to demonstrate strong leadership and management disciplines lacking in the club industry in Australia.
• The selection process used to attract, hire and select Michelle is one used by companies locally and globally. Telstra, PrioewaterhouseCoopers; Cisco Systems, Hewlett Packard, The Royal Bank of Scotland/Naf West and over 470 medium sized businesses in the UK last year used the Preferential Interviewing/Behavioural Interviewing approach to.recruit. The process has . been validated by legal expertise in Australian Industrial Relations. Tony was instrumental in sourcing/introducing this type of managerial expertise and skill development into the Club to ensure that hiring top quality staff became a priority.

THE DESTRUCTION OF CITY TATTERSALLS

- Has clearly demonstrated the ability to- create a structure and team which will ensure that the club has implemented sound business and commercial practice that will allow it to continue the fairly unique ability to trade profitably and successfully in an environment where evidence suggests the industry and competition is struggling significantly with the changes.
- In February through to June this year, he orchestrated revenue generating activities and strategies when the club faced a major downturn. Tony Guilfoyle was able to generate $700,000 trading which translated to $500,000 profit to the club. Currently the Club is trading with its best ever results in the harshest conditions in the Club's history.

The club is very clearly able to consolidate and build on its position in the market by making the appointment of Tony Guilfoyle to Chief Executive Officer immediately. From the job description and picture of the person needed to ensure the club's survival, subjectivity and randomness which can, on occasions cloud these types of decisions, are eliminated.

The remuneration package of $390,000 with bonus opportunities, leading to a $415,000 ceiling is consistent with the industry. Having discussed GM/CEO packages with key personnel from Robert Waters Recruitment and Executive Search, the average within the industry ranges from between $260.000 and $510,000 with appropriate bonus and performance incentives built in. These salaries are quite often dependant on percentage revenues from gaming versus other income generating sources. Packages for a CEO of a club like Revesbv Workers or Dee Whv would range from $430,000 and $390,000 respectively (with bonuses added on delivery of financial targets.)

In fact, in view of the nonperforming nature,of some of the

competition, the GM package demonstrates extraordinary value. With the outcomes/deliverables defined, the knowledge, skills and abilities/attitudes clearly detailed and demonstrated in behavioural terms, the decision becomes straightforward and virtually risk free.

Conclusion
It is vital for the board to make the decision on the appointment of Tony Guilfoyle to General Manager today. Any hesitation may well have disastrous implications by sending a message that services of Tony are not valued and/or needed. This could result in losing one of your most prized and well groomed managers, who is overwhelmingly capable of leading this fine club. The risk factor created by introducing an untried and untested outsider could not only undermine the many years of tradition but also result in irreparable damage to the implementation of the club's strategy in the future.

The Board has been consistently warned of difficult times and harsh trading conditions looming by Tony and have been presented with strategies and activities to maintain and enhance the revenue and profitability of the Club The recent figures reinforce the consistent achievement of the Clubs strongest ever trading results.

Over the next 7 years, the Club will be confronted with reacting to the impending taxation issues and jurisdictions that will have a major impact on downtown Sydney. Introducing an unfamiliar or untested candidate would be an act of complete folly and risk.

Tony Guilfoyle has a proven, enviable and tested track record of both leadership and delivery of consistent financial results, is respected and highly regarded within this industry and. will allow the Board to successfully affect a smooth transition of high quality management expertise and commercial acumen so critical for implementation in February 2004 for Silks CityTattersalls

So there you have it – how Tony Guilfoyle came to be CEO of City Tatts. We will return to this when you have had a chance to take it all in.
>Save City Tatts Committee
>Posted May 12, 2013 by savecitytatts

A Lesson in Organised Corruption

Members of City Tatts have rightly questioned how Tony Guilfoyle has been able to avoid the ongoing scrutiny that would be reasonably expected from the Chairman while pursuing his agenda of destroying the Club and selling out to private enterprise.

When Guilfoyle offically took over as CEO in February 2004 he had already assumed the majority of control in the Club for a number of years. He gradually expanded the responsibilities of his position as Assistant CEO. (His formula was to then retain the power and delegate the workload)

Now, as CEO, Guilfoyle wanted absolute power. To achieve this he knew he had to compromise those in the position of Chairman.

Compromising the Leaders
John Healy – Chairman No 1
When Guilfoyle became CEO John Healy was Chairman. Happily for Guilfoyle, Healy's position was already compromised. Healy was content to accept the occasional overseas trip, free meals, free parking and the $10,000 he was paid each year. The $10,000 was paid for supposedly "conducting gym classes". Other members conducted similar classes but only

By Tweedledum And Tweedledee

received free gym membership for their services.

Healy would dutifully present whatever Guilfoyle drafted for him at meetings and would sign off on the Guilfoyle-scripted "Chairman's Message" that appeared in the Club's Magazine. Healy was getting old and was easily manipulated by Guilfoyle.

John Kennedy – Chairman No 2
John Kennedy was the Committee's "next in line" under their succession plan for Chairman. When Guilfoyle became aware of the plan by John Kennedy and the other three trustees of the Bookmakers Superannuation Fund to implement a skim operation for their own benefit, he knew that if it went ahead he would have an automatic hold on Kennedy. In the middle of July 2004 Kennedy set up a bogus "promotion" company (Super Promoters Pty Ltd) to skim .615% off the assets of the BSF each year and then appointed Equity Trustees as trustee. For good measure Guilfoyle then merged the City Tattersalls Club Super Fund into the BSF (giving Kennedy an automatic benefit at the expense of the staff who were in the fund).

In 2008 Kennedy's bogus "promotion" company received $2 million from the fund but only spent $24,000 on Advertising and Promotion (a nice little earner).

The Member and Employer Representatives were never democratically elected and were always stooges from either senior management or the Club's Committee. Guilfoyle still retains a representative position to this day. Super Promoters is currently being investigated by ASIC and APRA.

Six months into his reign as CEO, with Healy and Kennedy in his pocket, Guilfoyle had no problem taking $200,000 from the Club without the permission of the Committee. Guilfoyle used this $200,000 to set up a business venture (Springs Resorts) with one of the Club's questionable consultants who has been paid in excess of $250,000 over the last few years (an obvious conflict of interest in itself).

When the $200,000 was brought to the attention of the Committee six years later (2010) it was covered up by Kennedy and current Chairman, Pat Campion. An investigation of this matter is currently under review by the Office of Liquor, Gaming and Racing.

Guilfoyle's incompetence, corruption and bullying went unchallenged by Kennedy with evidence showing he even supported it. Time caught up with Kennedy. For the last six months of his Chairmanship he could not face his "life long" friends in the gym when they became aware of the super fund ripoff (some of them lost heavily). Kennedy did not stand for re-election in 2011 and has not been sighted in the Club since.

Pat Campion – Chairman No 3
Guilfoyle assessed Campion's attitude on the Committee to be similar to most of the other Committee members. That is, accept without notice and without question whatever Guilfoyle put forward, put your hand up when required and sit down to a free lunch.

In 2007 Guilfoyle had to look at Campion differently. Kennedy was being groomed to take over from Healy as Chairman with Campion being endorsed as the next Vice Chairman. 2007 was a testing year for Guilfoyle. Too many members were becoming aware of his obvious mismanagement. He manouvered rule changes to take away members rights. He instigated a fear campaign about the impact of the non-smoking legislation to justify spending $7 million on the "Alfresco Gaming Hole" he proposed to put through the middle of the Club. He also had to convince members to approve the purchase of 194 Pitt Street for $9.25 million when the market value was no more than $6 million. Campion was a

By Tweedledum And Tweedledee

solicitor. What if he started to take his position seriously now that he was identified as a future Chairman? Guilfoyle was worried that Campion would learn that due diligence was either never carried out or ignored, because the building could never provide members what they were told to approve the purchase. The Club had bought a virtual derelict building that they would never be able to afford to refurbish.

At the same time as members were being asked to approve the purchase (Nov 2007) Guilfoyle organised for the Club to donate $80,000 to an arm of a charity that was chaired by Campion's brother. Members were misled to to believe that this $80,000 went directly to St John Ambulance (who in 2007 had a turnover of $20m, a marketing expense of $4m and a profit of $8m – the same year CTC ran at a loss). It was never disclosed to members that the $80,000 was used to fund an eye clinic in Moree (the Campion family's hometown) and it involved Campion's brother.

Guilfoyle now had Campion well and truly on the hook. Campion was now a willing servant of Guilfoyle.

Campion failed to act when he became aware of the conflict of interest when Guilfoyle formed Springs Resorts with a consultant that has been paid hundreds of thousands of dollars by Guilfoyle on behalf of the Club.

Campion failed to act when he became aware that Guilfoyle took $200,000 without the permission (or knowledge) of the then Committee in 2004.

Campion failed to act when he knew the $200,000 was a lump sum taken in 2004 and not the accumulation of travel and entertainment expenses that is being offset against accrued annual leave (the charade put up by Guilfoyle)

Campion was party to fabricated evidence in the Supreme Court action taken against the Club by a member.

Campion misled the recent AGM by informing members

that there were no legal settlements in 2011.
Campion did not disclose to members the $200,000 taken by Guilfoyle and is implicated in the cover-up.

The danger for members is that Guilfoyle and Campion will fast-track the sale of the Club premises hoping that skeletons of corruption will get buried in the demolition.

The plan by Guilfoyle and Campion is to present themselves to members as "White Knights", the saviours of the Club with a proposal – the Club has no alternative but sell out to developers and/or hoteliers. Ironic seeing that they were the main players in orchestrating the Club's deliberate demise.

>Save City Tatts Committee
>Posted November 18, 2012 by savecitytatts
>Tagged with Clinch Long Letherbarrow

City Tatts Forum
Archive for January, 2012.
City Tattersalls Club $80,000 Gift.
We have learned of a very strange donation by City Tattersalls Club.

This donation was for $80,000, was paid in 2007, and is quite interesting for a number of reasons.

The $80,000 was paid to an eye clinic in Moree, New South Wales run by Dr. Michael Campion.

Our understanding is that donations by registered clubs in NSW are intended to benefit their local community or, occasionally, recognised national appeals like the Red Cross. When did City Tattersalls Club start making donations to towns 600 kilometres away.

This donation to Moree was never disclosed to members

Donations made during the year are often mentioned in the Chairman's message. In fact, in that year the Chairman noted

By Tweedledum And Tweedledee

two donations of $25,000 each. But the $80,000 to the Moree eye clinic was never disclosed to members.

$80,000 is the biggest donation in recent memory by City Tattersalls Club. We are not aware of any other charitable donation exceeding even $40,000 in recent years.

The eye clinic in Moree is part of the St John Ambulance organisation

St John Ambulance is a large organisation that made a profit of $8 million in 2007. In the same year City Tattersalls Club made a loss. It seems very strange that City Tattersalls Club would give $80,000 to St John Ambulance.

As a general observation, if this is such a worthy project why didn't clubs in Moree and the surrounding area contribute the $80,000 ?

We would be very interested to hear more from members about this donation.

City Tattersalls Members Forum

Archive for March, 2012.

The Esperanto Restaurant - Another Financial disaster In City Tattersalls Club.

Following on from last week's blog about Zest Restaurant we realised that members would also like to know how the Esperanto Restaurant has traded in recent years.

Financial results for the Esperanto Restaurant

These are the trading results for the Esperanto based on answers given to various members at each AGM for the past few years -

. Year Ended 31 December 2006 $310,000 Loss
. Year Ended 31 December 2007 $390,000 Loss
. Year Ended 31 December 2008 $410,000 Loss
. Year Ended 31 December 2009 $350,000 Loss
. Year Ended 31 December 2010 $350,000 Loss

THE DESTRUCTION OF CITY TATTERSALLS

How is it possible for the Esperanto to lose so much money?
Just like Zest, the amount of money lost by the Esperanto is almost beyond belief. And remember, just like Zest, there is no rent to pay – you could probably add another $50,000 to the losses each year if the Club had to pay rent. We have discussed these results with experienced restaurant owners and operators and they simply can not understand how one restaurant can manage to lose so much money.

Who is in charge of restaurants in City Tattersalls Club?

While the Esperanto and Zest were losing money, the Food and Beverage manager in charge of them was paid a salary of almost $200,000 every year. In fact, in many of those years he got a bonus.

       City Tattersalls Members Forum

March 13, 2012
Zest Restaurant a financial disaster For City Tattersalls Club.
It occurred to us that very few members would know just how much money the Club has lost on Zest Restaurant. So here is some basic information to help you.

Zest Restaurant cost $2 million before it opened.

Zest Restaurant was part of the Zest/Lime Bar/Omega Lounge renovation that cost about $6 million in total. So Zest's share of this construction must be about $2 million (or more). Since the project involved abandoning the restaurant already in that space, it meant Zest needed to make additional profit of $2 million, over and above what the existing restaurant would make, to make financial sense.

How has Zest traded?
In the past few years a number of members have asked questions at the AGM about various financial aspects of the club including trading figures. Based on that, we have been able to

get a picture of how Zest has traded since it opened:
. Year Ended 31 December 2006 $540,000 Loss
. Year Ended 31 December 2007 $480,000 Loss
. Year Ended 31 December 2008 $520,000 Loss
. Year Ended 31 December 2009 $410,000 Loss
. Year Ended 31 December 2010 $380,000 Loss

Do you remember why the Smorgasbord closed?
Those of you with long memories will remember been told by management that they "had to" close the Smorgasbord because it was losing money. But even on management's figures the losses in it's final years, when it was allowed to deteriorate, were only about $200,000 a year. When you consider the incredible losses in Zest, the Smorgasbord looks better and better – especially when it was a real drawcard for the club.
      City Tattersalls Members Forum
March 10, 2012
Dining In At Tatts
Where do you get a reasonably priced meal in City Tattersalls Club?
One of the main benefits of being a member of a club, City Tatts or any other, is being able to get a good meal in a proper restaurant at a reasonable price. This used to be available in City Tatts but not any longer. There is simply nowhere in the club to get a reasonably priced meal.

A club needs a restaurant that appeals to a majority of members

The simple truth is that a club like City Tatts, which is run for the benefit of members, should have a restaurant that appeals to a majority of members. Obviously there isn't one now because the most members leave the club to eat elsewhere !

While it is fine to talk about opinions from surveys and the views of consultants, the ultimate verdict is always people's actions – and the members are clearly stating by their actions that they do not want what the club is offering.

Is Zest the answer?
The Club has made a big investment in Zest but is it really what members want?

There are a number of issues with Zest:

It is too expensive for most members – particularly if they want to eat in the club on a regular basis. While members might go to Zest for a special occasion, how many members will eat there every day?

Most members feel that the prices are too close to the Esperanto – it is not a realistic alternative for them. It has adversely affected the Esperanto by drawing a few customers from there rather than attracting new customers.

It seems to be an attempt to copy what city restaurants outside are offering. This has not worked for two reasons – A, it has no particular appeal to members. B, the club will surely lose in any head-to head competition with an owner-operated restaurant.

The size of the restaurant means that it needs to attract lots of customers to be viable – but there are not enough members who will pay those prices.

More and more customers are complaining about the quality of the food. In financial terms, it has been a disaster. A Buffet or Bistro is the obvious answer

Of all the possible types of restaurant that a club like City Tatts could offer, the ideal type is a buffet or bistro. It is no suprise that most clubs offer this.

A buffet has one competitive advantage - it enables the club to offer a good meal at a reasonable price, and then members will support it. It can do this because ordering at the counter reduces the staff required and offering lower prices ensures that the members use it. The strange part is that City Tatts had a buffet (and later a bistro – over Silks) that was very popular with members and visitors. In fact City Tatts did this better than most clubs because it offered a stylish eating area in a city centre location.

Archive for May, 2012.
Legal fees at City Tattersalls Club.
We have started to take a very keen interest in legal fees paid by City Tattersalls Club. And the more we look the more we find. Let's just look at one case that we know of.
What the Club told members about legal fees during 2011?
Like all clubs, City Tatts is required by the Registered Clubs Act to disclose details of any legal fees paid by the Club on behalf of a Committee member or employee. According to the disclosures issued to members there were none in 2011.
Also, at the Annual General Meeting of the Club last week, members asked if there were any legal settlements or legal fees paid for Committee members or employees in 2011. Again, the Chairman told the meeting that there were none.

May 6, 2012
What Happens To all The money At City Tattersalls Club?
There is plenty of money in City Tatts – the problem is where it is being spent. One of the biggest areas of waste is legal fees.

Legal Fees at City Tattersalls Club.
These are the amounts spent on legal fees for the past 7 years, all to Bartier Perry:
Year Ended 31 December 2005 $79,819
Year Ended 31 December 2006 $72,293
Year Ended 31 December 2007 $232,588

Year Ended 31 December 2008 $71,900
Year Ended 31 December 2009 $66,285
Year Ended 31 December 2010 $185,187
Year Ended 31 December 2011 $195,899

This is madness!

Spending $903,971 on legal fees in seven years is simply madness. City Tatts is a members club whose only function is to provide facilities and amenities to members. Any club spending this kind of money on legal fees is clearly doing something wrong. Just think of what the Club could have done for members with this money.

The Esperanto Room - How Long Will It be there?
Esperanto's losses are staggering.

As detailed in previous posts, the losses at the Esperanto are staggering. The latest figures given to members who asked, show that it lost another $400 000 in 2011. This follows five consecutive years of losses of $300 000 or worse each year.

It's hard to understand how it is possible to lose so much money. They have no rent to pay, the food servings are small and they charge plenty. But, whatever the reason, with losses on that scale, and no sign of improvement, it is possible that closure is being considered.

July 31, 2012
City Tattersalls Club - A Friend's Place.

City Tatts has been a friends' place since Tony Guilfoyle became CEO in 2004. Georgeson Architects certainly think so.

Georgeson Associates – Architects

Georgeson Architects have done very well out of City Tatts. They have received over $600,000 since 2006. That is just their fees, not counting any materials or construction cost. That in

By Tweedledum And Tweedledee

itself tells you a lot about the Club in recent years.

Unfortunately City Tatts has not done nearly as well from the relationship. Building works have been one of the worst areas of waste and mismanagement in the Club over the past eight years. Most of the projects were failures to begin with, from the point of view of members. Zest restaurant is an obvious example. It cost millions to refurbish and was a flop from day one, which would have been obvious to anyone with any brains. But apart from faulty proposals the construction project management has also been seriously flawed.

There has been continual mismanagement in the construction program since 2004. Again and again we see a new project where the first task is to pull down work completed only three or fours years before. To take just one example – how many attempts have there been since 2004 to do a proper entrance and they still can't get it right? Most members say that the latest entrance is the worst ever (see previous blogs) – and it will cost $1.1 million. Georgeson Architects have been involved in most of these botched building jobs but we don't know whether the problem is their incompetence or faulty instructions from management.

Georgeson's were also the architects on the renovation of Boonoona Ski Lodge which is owned by City Tatts.

Another Friends' Place

Georgeson Architects have done well in other ways from the City Tatts connection. They were also the architects for the construction of Springs Resorts Mittagong which is located beside Mittagong RSL. Springs

Resorts Mittagong is owned by Tony Guilfoyle. They also acted as architects for Tony Guilfoyle's house extension in Cronulla. This was a substantial renovation costing $750,000.

We just hope that Tony Guilfoyle got better value for his

money than City Tatts!
> City Tattersalls Members Forum

August 20, 2012
City Tattersalls Club In the Sydney Morning Herald.

By now, most of you would know about the two articles in Saturday's Sydney Morning Herald.

We haven't laughed this much in years!

Here at the City Tattersalls Members Forum we have been laughing since we read the paper on Saturday morning. Obviously, the issues mentioned in the stories were not news to us, or indeed to any concerned member, so that's not why we're laughing.

No, what made us laugh were the responses by Patrick Campion and Tony Guilfoyle when the issues were put to them. Overall these two have provided the most hilarious response to issues of mismanagement that we have ever seen from any Chairman or Chief Executive – not just in a club but in any organisation. We are laughing so much that we don't know where to start. But we are going to try.

September 11, 2012
Payments to City Tatts Club Boss?

Here is another gem from the Sydney Morning Herald articles about City Tattersalls Club: "I have not taken money without the board knowing"

This is what Tony Guilfoyle said when questioned about the $200,000 that he owes to City Tatts.

He also said that it was not a loan. Apparently Patrick Campion agreed with both of these statements. Rather than give our opinion, maybe we should ask the auditors.

What KPMG say about the Guilfoyle loan.

By Tweedledum And Tweedledee

Here is what the auditors, KPMG, say: KPMG say that the money was paid to Guilfoyle and that "this does not appear to have been formally approved by the Committee!!"

KPMG recommended that the amount owed by Guilfoyle be "approved by the Committee annually including appropriate terms for repayment". KPMG recommended that "the balance owing to the Club be disclosed in the notes to the financial statements."

Is it just us or does that sound like a loan that was not approved by the Committee!

KPMG must go!

Now we come to the crux of the matter.

If Guilfoyle and Campion really believe what they say then KPMG must go!

Please understand that this is not our opinion – but it is the only logical opinion the Club could have. Just think about it. KPMG are paid $80,000 a year for the audit. And, according to Guilfoyle and Campion, KPMG are completely wrong in their view of the Guilfoyle loan. If they are so incompetent, on such a simple matter, then how could the Club continue to employ them as auditors?

City Tattersalls Members Forum

Archive for November, 2012.
City Tattersalls Club - Racquetball Courts Renamed!

Patrick Campion's recent Chairman's Message did provide one very funny titbit of information. It seems that two of the racquetball courts are to be renamed – one after John Healy and one after Kevin Smith!

Certainly, if you had to pick two names to symbolise the shocking decline of City Tatts, you could not have picked two better names.

THE DESTRUCTION OF CITY TATTERSALLS

As has been well documented on the internet, John Healy is the one most responsible for starting the decline of City Tatts. He was the Chairman who proposed Tony Guilfoyle for the CEO job and continued to support him even when members realised that he was running the Club into the ground. Healy also set new low standards for dealing with members that are still being followed today.

Kevin Smith is a perfect example of the Committee in City Tatts – he has closed his eyes to every disaster that has happened to the Club in the past eight years. He has watched as restaurants failed, entertainment ceased and consultants got rich while the Club edged closer to bankruptcy. Not once has he taken a stand against the destruction of the Club. Close observers of the Club had said that he was planning to retire from the Committee. This racquetball move might be designed to keep him there one more year – which would suit Pat Campion and Tony Guilfoyle much better than a new Committee member who might question the obvious mismanagement of the Club.

       City Tattersalls Members Forum

Archive for December, 2012.
The Bookmakers Superannuation Fund And City Tattersalls Club.
Now that the Bookmakers Superannuation Fund is back in the news, courtesy of another article in the Australian Financial Review, it might be a good time to mention another mattter that was never resolved – the Supreme Curt case involving City Tatts.

What caused the Supreme Court case?
The Supreme Court case arose when a member of City Tatts wrote to the Committee suggesting that John Kennedy

should be stood down as Chairman pending an investigation into his role in the Bookmakers Superannuation Fund "promotion" scheme.

Even back then this was a fairly reasonable request, and subsequent revelations about the Bookmakers Superannuation Fund proved that it was well founded. But this is City Tatts – so two days later the Committee moved to expel the member! For the record, Patrick Campion fully supported this move to expel the member.

In case you are wondering why the member was so concerned about Kennedy's role in the Bookmakers Superannuation Fund, the following are just some of the ways it impacted on City Tatts:

. The Bookmakers Superannuation Fund had it's office on the second floor of City Tatts for many years.

. Employees of City Tatts were encouraged by senior management to put their super into the Bookmakers Superannuation Fund. And employees who had their super in the City Tatts Staff Super Fund found out that their fund had been rolled into the Bookmakers Superannuation Fund anyway! (To this day, many are fuming about this).

Many members of City Tatts have their super in the Bookmakers Superannuation Fund, and were not happy when they realised what Kennedy had done. (This is why Kennedy did not seek re-election in 2011 – in fact he had avoided all contact with members for at least six months before that)

We look forward to the next step in this saga.

City Tattersalls Members Forum

Archive for April, 2013.
Rule Changes Proposed By City Tatts Members.
Back in February members submitted eight rule changes to protect the Club. The saga of these proposed rule changes is

a perfect illustration of how City Tatts has been run in recent years by Pat Campion and Tony Guilfoyle.

These rule changes were submitted in February to give the Committee plenty of time to have them dealt with along with the Annual General Meeting on May 21, at practically no cost to members. But the Committee has decided to have a separate meeting on June 25 to deal with them.

What makes this remarkable is that in 2010 the Committee led by John Kennedy (with Pat Campion as his deputy) lamented the cost of having a separate meeting ($30,000 according to him) to discuss rule changes. (But Kennedy had no problem whatsoever with the Club spending $60,000 in the same year to send him and a few favoured employees to Hong Kong, Macau and Singapore – that cost was not even worth a mention.) It is obvious that the Committee did not want these rule changes discussed at the AGM and was willing to spend members money to prevent that.

But it gets worse – because the Committee has refused to allow five of the eight changes to even be put to members. This is completely contrary to the rules but it is a perfect example of how City Tatts is run now. Anytime the Committee don't want to do something, even if it is required by the rules, they run to Bartier Perry who supply the legal advice to support what the Committee wants. Bartier Perry might think they are untouchable but someday they will be brought to account for their role in the decline of City Tatts.

And then the final insult, to make sure that there is no doubt about what the Committee thinks of members. Of the three rule changes being put to members, the Committee "will not be supporting" even these three proposals – ie. they are against them. So, in summary, here are eight fairly reasonable rule changes proposed by members to protect the Club – and the Committee are opposed to all eight.

By Tweedledum And Tweedledee

These are the eight proposed rule changes:
Rule Change 1 and 2 – Delete Rules 4.2 (p) (q) and (r).
The current rules 4.2 (q) and (r) are the most dangerous rules we have ever seen in any Club. The first one allows the Committee to delegate any of its powers to anyone. Incredibly, the second one allows that person to delegate those powers to anyone else. You can see how this would be useful if you wanted to hand over the Club's premises to a property developer without interference from those pesky members.

Rule Change 3
This is a fairly simple proposal to have the names on the ballot papers in random order rather than in alphabetical order as it is now.

Rule Change 4
This change is probably the most important of the eight.

Rule 17.1 (a)(1) notwithstanding the provisions of the Registered Clubs Act and Rules the Committee sahll not enter intoa contract or agrteement in relationtoanyClub property, with anyCommittee member, Club member, Club employee or their family members, relatives, or legal entities ot trusts, unless the proposed dealing is approved by the members passing a special resolution at a General Meeting.

This one would have been a major stumbling block to the Committee's property plans, so they were afraid to let members even see it, never mind let them vote on it.

Rule Change 5
This was a very simple rule change to allow members to ap-

point a scrutineer for ballots on resolutions, in the same way that members can presently appoint scrutineers for ballots for Committee elections.

Rule Change 6
This rule change would have required the Committee to apply the rules of natural justice and the laws of New South Wales in making decisions.

Naturally, the Committee are totally opposed to this – and refused to allow members to vote on it!

Rule Change 7
This rule change would allow 100 members to call a General Meeting. The Committee will allow members to vote on this one – but they don't support it.

Rule Change 8
This rule change would require the Club to provide a full transcript of General Meetings of members to any member who requested it. This is necessary to overcome the present situation where the Committee has access to the transcripts of meetings but members are denied access.

City Tattersalls Members Forum

Well, it has just got worse.
Patrick Campion has granted a mortgage over 194 Pitt Street to ANZ Bank!
As many of you would know, the City Tattersalls Club Act makes it illegal to mortgage the Club's property without the approval of members at a general meeting. You would think that Campion, a solicitor, would know that.

We knew that National Australia Bank were having a very close look at City Tatts so it is no surprise that something has happened in this area. It could be that ANZ are hoping to profit from the "airspace" development.

Members will need to act soon if they want to save their Club. Stop any member of the Committee, if you are lucky enough to see them in the Club, and question them about this. They may not even know it has happened.

    City Tattersalls Members Forum

December 30, 2013
The Promotions Department At City Tatts.

We were told recently that there are 5 people working full time in the promotions department at City Tatts.

This was hard to believe but we checked and it is correct. (You might be interested to know that the Bowlers Club in York Street has 5 people in their office to run the whole club.)

This started us thinking about the benefits to members of all that promotion.

First there is the cost. Apart from the wages of these 5 people there is the added cost of radio advertising and various other promotions, most of which are failures. And for the past year or so there has been an outside "consultant" whose real job is to handle criticism from members. And sure enough if you look at the annual accounts you'll see that the total cost of all this promotion was $2.2 million in 2012.

The second part of assessing the promotions department is to look at the results of their efforts. Basically their efforts have resulted in total failure. The falling membership alone tells the whole story. Membership has fallen by more than 50%, from 34,000 to about 15,000 since 2004. Takings at the Club's bars and restaurants have also fallen, confirming the absolute failure of this department. Even poker machine takings are falling.

And then you have to ask – what exactly could they be promoting? There is no entertainment in the Club. The restaurants would not attract anyone. Zest is a hopeless failure, rejected by members as soon as it opened. Cafe 2 is a joke – only kept open because members won't go to Zest. As for the Esperanto, let's be honest – it appeals to about 1% of members.

So even if their promotions did get someone to go to the club, why would anyone come back?

The answer is obvious – get rid of this department, cancel the radio advertising – and spend this $2.2 million in ways that directly benefit members.

City Tattersalls Members Forum

30 December 2013
Questions About The City Tatts Property Plan
One of the unanswered questions about the proposed development is the cost of fitting out the floors the Club will get. We are indebted to a member who asked a question at the end of the meeting on 10 December 2013.

He asked about the cost of the fit-out and whether the Club would have to pay for this, and, if so, how?

We are not sure what Patrick Campion said in reply. The consensus was that he said something about it being too early to give detailed answers on this.

But this is a very important question.

Under the proposed plan, the Club will be in a precarious position anyway. If it has to spend $10 million to fit out it's own floors then it has no chance.

City Tattersalls Members Forum

21 January 2014
Parking At City Tattersalls Club
There was a slight hitch at the December 10 meeting called as part of the publicity campaign to convince members that a

By Tweedledum And Tweedledee

property development was the way forward for the Club.

The hitch came when members asked a few questions about the proposal. Interestingly, the most common concern was the lack of parking in the building for anyone who buys one of the units. John Chomley from Colliers tried to convince the meeting that parking was not necessary but no one was convinced. One gent from the country said that without parking he simply would not buy a unit in the development.

The truth is that Colliers (and Mirvac) would love to have parking but they know the council will not allow it. So they are trying to put a brave face on the situation. Just have a look at residential developments around the city, or talk to buyers, and you will find out how important parking is. Even Mirvac admit that the lack of parking makes the units less attractive.

The other hitch was when a member reminded the meeting that Patrick Campion had mortgaged the Club's building to ANZ bank without the approval of members, thereby breaching the City Tattersalls Club Act. Now, this will prove to be a major stumbling block to any development.

City Tattersalls Members Forum

Radio Advertising
One of the very interesting facts to emerge from financial questions was that radio advertising cost $246,000 in 2011. This is interesting because when members asked a few years ago it was $500,000 and a few years before that it was $900,000 (yes, $900,000 in one year, that is not a misprint).

We have known for a long time that the money spent on radio advertising was a disgraceful waste of members' funds but in their own roundabout way the Club has now basically admitted this. Just consider a few basic facts about radio advertising at City Tatts:

City Tatts used to spend $900,000 a year on radio advertising but once members started asking questions about it the amount has dropped every year. This makes no sense. If it was money well spent it would make no difference whether members asked about it or not. Clearly, the scrutiny from members exposed it for the fraud it always was.

Every time members asked about it, management have always assured them that it was successful, that they were pleased with it, that it was effective etc. etc. The problem is that the same answers were given whether they were spending $900,000, $500,000 or $246,000. It is not possible that spending $900,000 or $246,000 is equally valuable. If spending $900,000 was bringing great benefits to the Club, then they are making a big mistake today in only spending $246,000. If spending $246,000 is enough, then the excess $654,000 was a disgraceful waste. Either they were lying back then or they are lying now.

In any case, it is clear from listening to the answers at the AGM that management have no idea if radio advertising brings any benefit to the Club. Any club that spends $900,000 on anything should be able to clearly demonstrate the benefit to the club or else you don't spend it !

Apart from the nonsense "explanations" provided by management, it is obvious to members that spending hundreds of thousands of dollars on radio advertising is a complete waste of members' money. Here is our simple suggestion: Cancel all radio advertising today and give the money directly to members in door prizes, free drinks and subsidised meals. This would have ten times the promotional impact.

194 Pitt Street

194 Pitt Street is always of interest to us (and should be of interest to all members who care about their club) because

it has been a financial disaster from the day it was bought in 2007 and nothing has changed since. Questions at the meeting reminded us of a few issues about the building.

It is not possible for City Tattersalls Club to trade so badly?
It doesn't take a genius to see that City Tatts is struggling. But it is only when you dig a little deeper that the scale of the disaster becomes clear. Basically, the Club has performed so badly since 2004 that it can only be intentional. There is no conceivable incompetence, inefficiency or mismanagement that could produce results this bad.
Just consider the situation Guilfoyle inherited in 2004. City Tatts had thrived for 100 years through recession, depression and world war. It owned a large building in the best possible location in Sydney. It had restaurants, bars, gyms and other facilities that were much appreciated by its loyal members. The population living in the city was growing every year. And one more thing – yes, it had over 400 poker machines making a profit of $24 million every year.

What has happened since then is beyond belief.
Everything he has touched has failed. Every building project has failed. Every restaurant is failing. (It is not possible for a restaurant to lose $400,000 every year, when you have no rent to pay.) It has been an 8 year track record of total failure.
How did he get away with failure for so long?
You have to wonder why the Committee let him get away with this for so long. Even the members knew as early as 2006 that he was a complete idiot. One reason is that he always took special care to look after the Chairman. We have provided extensive information in previous blogs on Save City Tatts about the three Club Chairmen since 2004. Here it is only necessary to point out that all three were receiving something

from the Club that seems to have made them reluctant to rock the boat. So John Healy got his overseas trip and $10,000 a year for gym classes (even though others doing similar classes got nothing). John Kennedy was allowed to run the Bookmakers Superannuation Fund skim operation, making millions for him and the other Three Amigos. And a clinic in Moree which just happens to be run by Pat Campion's brother gets a donation of $80,000 from City Tatts, but the members of City Tatts are never told.

194 Pitt Street is the key to this sordid tale
More and more it looks like buying 194 Pitt Street is the key to understanding the real game. Other internet blogs provide a detailed account of the purchase. In a nutshell, it has been an unmitigated disaster from the point of view of members. Given that members got nothing from the purchase you have to look at what they were told when they approved the purchase. Most of the promises made to members turned out to be false. For instance, the promised cafe. restaurant and administration office were instantly rejected by the council. This leads you to question the due diligence supposedly done prior to purchase. Basically, either no due diligence was done or it was totally negligent.

But when you look at the purchase from the point of view of someone who wants to hand the Club's property to a developer at a later date it starts to make sense. For one thing, the $9.8 million debt burden instantly increased the odds of the Club getting into financial difficulties and being "forced" to sell it's building. Buying 194 Pitt Street also does a lot directly for the developers, giving them additional options to maximise their profit.

The timetable for selling the building
Members fear that the storm clouds gathering over Tony

By Tweedledum And Tweedledee

Guilfoyle will prompt the parties to bring forward the plan to sell the building:

He is under investigation by the Department of Gaming & Racing over the $200,000 he took from the Club, without approval of the Committee. (Not that they could have approved it anyway – loans to employees are prohibited by the Club Rules.)

T he relentless exposure on the internet of his dismal failure is getting harder to ignore.

He is trying to sell his motels in Nowra and Mittagong, so he may have money problems.

A few senior employees who were always considered to be on Guilfoyle's side now seem to be discreetly preparing for his departure. (Basically he bought their loyalty with members' money by paying them twice what they would have got elsewhere.) We interpret this as an obvious plan to distance themselves from him for when the proverbial hits the fan.

Even the Committee of City Tatts are starting to doubt him.

(Here at Save City Tatts we had extreme difficulty believing this. We have watched for years as the Committee let him do whatever he wanted without a squeak out of them. But careful observers of the Club say they have detected the very early signs of the Committee turning against him. As a small example they notice that the level of propaganda in the Club magazine has declined significantly in recent issues.)

Who are the players in the game?

Reports from inside and outside the Club have identified the frontrunners in the race to get control of the Club's prized asset – it's property. Last year a meeting was held in March in the Club between a well-known hotelier, a person holding high profile racing positions, a financier and a former City Tatts Treasurer. There have been further meetings and the

Club Corruption Vigilante is certain that the property is now "in play".
>Save City Tatts Committee
>Posted November 18, 2012 by savecitytatts

Trouble at Balmain Leagues Club – Could the same happen at City Tattersalls Club?
That was a very interesting story on the weekend on the front page of the Sydney Morning Herald about the financial problems at Balmain Leagues Club. Naturally we wondered if the same could happen at City Tattersalls Club.
What happened at Balmain Leagues Club
Let's summarise what happened at Balmain Leagues Club and use it as a blueprint, or template, for what could happen at City Tatts:
A club gets into financial difficulties and owes a lot of money. Someone close to the club comes up with a plan to "save" the club. This plan is presented to members as the only option to save the club.
The "saviour", whose only concern is to save the club, just happens to make millions from the "rescue" – always from redeveloping the club's property..(Property is the key.)

Could it happen at City Tattersalls Club?
With this blueprint in mind, let's look at the present state of City Tatts:
City Tatts has been badly run for years and now owes a lot of money (about $20 million to National Australia Bank alone). It was particularly interesting to read that Balmain Leagues Club was "bleeding ... through previous risky property acquisitions and declining patronage of it's poker machines". Sound familiar?

By Tweedledum And Tweedledee

We have every confidence that many of the people presently doing so well from City Tatts would be delighted to come up with a plan to "save" the Club. Here we are thinking of top management, builders, consultants and one or two on the Committee. (You only have to think back to John Kennedy's role in the Bookmakers Fund, where he generously agreed to roll all of the City Tattersalls Club Staff Super fund into the BSF, which just happened to increase his own income).

City Tatts owns a prime CBD property and we know that the Committee have dreamed about redeveloping the City Tatts site for a long time. John Healy used to talk about putting a hotel on the site. We would expect that any property developer who made millions on the redevelopment would be very grateful to any insider who could deliver the property to them. Realistically, isn't this where City Tattersalls Club is heading? When you look at how City Tatts has gone since Tony Guilfoyle became CEO, you have to worry that the Club is heading the way of Balmain Leagues Club. Even back in 2006, many members speculated that his real agenda must be to run the Club into the ground. They came to this conclusion by simply observing his actions as CEO. He inherited a thriving club with a fantastic location, great facilities, and loyal members and with every major decision or project he has taken the Club closer to collapse. Even a complete idiot would have got a few right by pure chance.

    Save City Tatts Committee
    Posted November 18, 2012 by savecitytatts

Artwork at City Tattersalls Club!
Some of you may have noticed new paintings around City Tatterssals Club. As with everything else in the club. there is more to this than meets the eye.

THE DESTRUCTION OF CITY TATTERSALLS

City Tattersalls Club pays $54 000 to display these paintings
Thanks to members who asked questions at the recent AGM, we now have some information on the arrangement, in particular that City Tatts pays $54 000 a year to have these paintings displayed.

From what we have been able to find out, it seems that these paintings belong to some Aboriginal art gallery and while on display at City Tatts are available for sale. If a member does happen to buy one, the gallery makes a commision and the artists gets what's left.

And for providing a showroom for the gallery- City Tatts pays them????

This seems like a really good deal for the gallery and the person that introduced it to the City Tatts Club, but it certainly has no benefit to the Club or the members. This has only created more unreasonable and unjustifaible spending by the management and the committee.

>Save City Tatts Committee
>Posted November 18, 2012 by savecitytatts

How Food and Beverage actually performed in 2011.
These are the the facts of how Food and Beverage performed at City Tatts in 2011, which emerged only because members specifically demanded the information under the Club's Rules: Food and Beverage at City Tatts lost $650,000 in 2011.

The Esperanto restaurant lost $400,000 in 2011. That is not a misprint – it actually lost $400,000. In fact, it managed to lose $409,000 on sales of $919,000. When you realise that they have no rent to pay, that might make it the worst restaurant performance in Sydney. Obviously, looking at these figures would cause anyone to question management's ability, to put it mildly. But we have checked with people in the restaurant trade and they have told us that even total stupidity would not produce results this bad. And Jimmy Chen? He doesn't even mention it. Maybe he doesn't know.

Zest restaurant lost $300,000 in 2011.
They even manage to lose money on beverage. The Esperanto managed to lose $105,000, and Zest managed to lose $82,000, on beverage alone ! Since the Club would charge customers, on average, twice or even three times it's cost price, this also must be some kind of record for losing money.
Remember, they "had to" close the Smorgasbord because it was losing money. In the three years that Jimmy Chen has been Treasurer, the Club's top two restaurants have lost a combined $2,200,000 !
The other notable point about the Esperanto and Zest is that they are not cheap. If the meals were being given away at half-price you could understand some losses. But they are charging top dollar for everything, which makes these losses all the more inexplicable.

This is not acceptable!
To tell members that revenue has risen and make no mention of the horrendous losses during the year, or indeed for the past seven years, is a disgraceful attempt to mislead members. Besides, what is the point of increasing revenue if you are losing money on every meal?
   Save City Tattersalls Committee.
   Posted November 18, 2012 by savecitytatts

City Tattersalls Club – big salaries for no results (Part 1)
Money is being wasted left, right and centre at City Tatts.
Nowhere is there greater waste than in the inflated salaries given to top management for dismal performance. Here is an

THE DESTRUCTION OF CITY TATTERSALLS

introduction to where members money is being wasted on salaries.

Tony Guilfoyle

Guilfoyle has been a failure as CEO from day one. Almost everything he has tried has been a flop. If you were to examine his top 10 projects as CEO, whether restaurants, building jobs, property purchases or just general management duties, you would find that 9 of them are failures, sometimes hilariously so. In fact, you will have to look hard to find the one that is a success. But a track record of failure is no longer a barrier for top management at City Tatts. Instead they get increases and bonuses. Here is what City Tatts has paid Guilfoyle since he became CEO -

Year Ended 31 December 2004	$410,000
Year Ended 31 December 2005	$410,000
Year Ended 31 December 2006	$430,000
Year Ended 31 December 2007	$430,000
Year Ended 31 December 2008	$460,000
Year Ended 31 December 2009	$530,000
Year Ended 31 December 2010	$540,000
Year Ended 31 December 2011	$540,000

Some things about City Tatts are so strange that it is no wonder people don't believe them when they are told for the first time. Here is someone who clearly has no ability of any kind to run the Club and yet he has been given $3,750,000 in 8 years. And the best part is – he is only there 3 days a week!

Patrick Campion – a study in weakness

When John Kennedy decided not to run again, because of the rising anger over his role in the Bookmakers Superannuation Fund, he was replaced by Patrick Campion. Campion, a solicitor, had been the Vice Chairman under Kennedy and had been on the Committee since 2005. Campion's key personality trait is that he is weak. He never really takes a stand on anything – he just goes along with whatever others have decided. There is no record of him ever standing up for members. Campion;s track record – before becoming Chairman

Since Campion's time on the Committee coincides exactly with the the decline of City Tattersalls Club we need to have a closer look at his track record:

First and foremost, since he joined the Committee, Campion has gone along with everything that Tony Guilfoyle has done to the Club. And that means everything. Every reduction in member amenities, every bit of waste (fees to consultants, overseas trips, legal fees etc), every failed project (Zest, the Coffee Cart, 194 Pitt Street etc) – you name it, Campion supported Guilfoyle om it. Not once did he question anything. And it also means that he voted for every pay increase and bonus that Guilfoyle has ever received.

Campion blindly followed John Healy and John Kennedy on everything they did to restrict or remove the rights of members trying to save the Club.

Campion was on the Committee when a donation of $80,000 was paid to a clinic in Moree run by his brother, Michael Campion (but never disclosed to members).

Campion was Vice Chairman when he, along with most of the Committee, discovered that an employee had taken over $200,000 without their knowledge. Naturally Pat decided to do nothing about it.

     Save City Tatts Committee
     Posted November 16, 2012

Patrick Campion's "new Banking Arrangements."
More from the Chairman's Message in the latest City Tatts magazine.

THE DESTRUCTION OF CITY TATTERSALLS

After it was reported on internet blogs that the Club had moved from NAB to ANZ, Pat Campion had to come clean and say something about it to members.

We expected Campion to conceal the real story from members – and he did. But the way he went about this was comical, even by Campion standards. In fact, we had to read the passage a few times to understand the Campion explanation. The Campion explanation is that NAB wanted to put a mortgage over all the Club's property. The Committee didn't want this so they decided to go to ANZ – and then gave ANZ a mortgage over all the Club's property!

You can see why we had to read it a few times.

Of course, as usual, members have not been told the real story. The reality is that NAB got so worried about how the Club was being run that they feared their loans might not be repaid and wanted a mortgage over the Club's main building, not just 194 Pitt St.

And, as previously mentioned, under the City Tattersalls Act any new mortgage must be approved in advance by members. Campion didn't bother with this minor detail.

>Save City Tatts Committee
>Posted May 5, 2013 by savecitytatts

Patrick Campion and the Office of Liquor Gaming and Racing investigation.

In the latest City Tatts magazine Pat Campion tells members that the investigation by the Office of Liquor Gaming & Racing into Tony Guilfoyle is finalised and that there were no adverse findings against Tony Guilfoyle or the Club.

He also said the investigation was an expensive and time-wasting distraction.

Yes, it was – entirely due to Pat Campion.

When Pat Campion and the rest of the Committee found out

that Tony Guilfoyle had taken $200,000 without the knowledge or approval of the Committee there should have been immediate action. Instead Pat Campion turned a blind eye and also concealed it from members. Even the Club's auditor wanted the unauthorised loan disclosed to members. The only reason for the OLGR investigation was because Pat Campion refused to do anything.

As for expense, again Pat Campion is totally responsible for this. It was his decision to get the Club's solicitors, Bartier Perry, to deal with OLGR at enormous expense to the Club. Of course, the advantage of getting Bartier Perry to deal with OLGR is that Pat Campion and Tony.

Michelle Abbey – Million Dollar Baby!

Michelle Abbey was the first high profile appointment by Guilfoyle after he became CEO. She was paid an insane salary of $250,000 per year as Marketing Director and was a total failure. In the four years she was at the Club she received a cool $1 million. She would not have brought in enough revenue to cover her own salary, never mind contribute anything to the Club.

She is also a perfect example of everything that has gone wrong with City Tatts. The whole notion of a Marketing Director on $250,000 at City Tattersalls Club is ridiculous. The Club's facilities, location and tradition provide all the promotion necessary. City Tatts was a thriving club for years without any Marketing Director. And, with the greatly increased population living in the city centre, it should be doing even better now.

There is another reason why paying someone $250,000 a year to promote the Club is nonsense. At the same time that Guilfoyle hired her to promote the Club, he started to take away the very things that used to bring people to the Club! So the

Smorgasboard (probably the Club's greatest attraction) was closed down, Then entertainment was reduced and eventually stopped. Other restaurants and bars were closed before spending millions on new restaurants and bars that members rejected. It simply makes no sense to pay huge salaries to attract people to the Club while you remove the very things that have proven in the past to attract people to the Club.

Members are being deceived in other ways by these insane salaries. By paying someone $250,000 a year, Guilfoyle is trying to convince everyone that City Tatts is a large complex business that is difficult to run. In fact, it is a very simple operation that anyone could run using basic common sense. If you stopped somebody at random walking past the front door they would run the Club better than it is now.

Jan Elks

Jan Elks is Guilfoyle's secretary. We are not sure what her qualifications were to get the job but it should be a fairly easy job given that Guilfoyle is only there three days a week on average. But this is City Tatts, so it will not surprise you to learn that she is now paid $135,000 a year ! That's right – City Tatts pays Jan Elks $135,000 a year.

This is how members' money is being wasted. Do you really think that Jan Elks would get $135,000 a year if Kevin Smith or Bill Hurley were paying it from their own pockets ? Not a chance – but if members are paying it (and the members don't know) then don't worry about it. Incidentally, we have checked around the CBD and the maximum salary for what she actually does is $50,000. So, how much has she been overpaid in the five years she's been there – $200,000? $300,000? How's that for waste ?

        Save City Tatts Committee
        Posted November 18, 2012 by savecitytatts

By Tweedledum And Tweedledee

Insanity on a large scale.

You have to admire the committee at City Tatts. Their capacity to do nothing in the face of disaster is staggering.

Just stop and think about this "airspace" project. This is the latest plan from a clown whose previous plans have all failed. Every one.

One of Tony Guilfoyle's tactics to hide his incompetence has been to engage in a perpetual building program – which has been a disaster in every way.

Take the Zest/Omega/Lime Bar project as an example. This was Guilfoyle's biggest project to date so naturally it has been his biggest failure to date. The whole project cost $6 million (or $7 million – building costs tend to blow out at City Tatts) and has proved a disaster in every way.

In fact, just looking at Zest, it was already a failure at the design stage. That's because he decided to spend $2 million on a new restaurant when there already was a restaurant in that space. And before the bistro it had been the Corinthian Room. (Actually the Corinthian Room had some style, unlike Zest which is just dull.) Also, it was madness to have a new expensive restaurant when the Esperanto already served that market. But of course the committee eat for free so prices are irrelevant. But members gave their verdict within a few weeks of opening.

So the insane waste on building Zest was only the start. Since it opened in 2006 it has lost more than $3 million. That is not a misprint – Zest, a restaurant with no rent to pay, has lost more than $3 million since 2006. So just one crackpot decision about one new restaurant has cost members at least $5 million.

And now this clown is going to attempt to develop an apartment block. And what will that involve? That's right, he is going to rebuild Zest – again! And rebuild the Lime Bar

– again! And the Omega lounge? It looks like the Omega lounge (which must have cost about $2 million) is gone! So basically most of the Zest/Omega/Lime Bar construction will be ripped out.

Now the mystery is why the committee allow Guilfoyle to do anything, never mind a property development. Make no mistake, when he fails with a $100 million project like this, as is certain, it will be the end of City Tatts. Well, it seems that as many as half of the committee have finally realised that he has been a disaster – but they are going to stick with him. They know that to get rid of him now would be admitting they made a huge mistake years ago. And, of course, a new CEO would expose evrything that the committee has turned a blind eye to.

So they believe the best course, for them, is to proceed with a property development even if it is a disaster. They feel that's the best way to cover up their role in the destruction of the club.

>Save City Tatts Committee
>Posted March 24, 2014 by savecitytatts

The property development at Balmain Leagues Club
Anyone who thinks a property development will save City Tatts should have a good look at Balmain Leagues Club.
The Balmain Leagues Club redevelopment "was dealt a potentially fatal blow on Wednesday when the NSW government's Planning and Infrastructure Department rejected the existing plan because of traffic concerns". As a result "it is unlikely any major development will happen on this site".
In particular, the RTA noted "increased queuing and severe congestion on the road network surrounding the site".
And, if that wasn't bad enough, the developer also lent millions to the club to allow it to keep operating. Of course this

allowed the developer to apply to have a receiver appointed to the club. (This was always bound to happen.) The application has been delayed by an injunction granted by the Supreme Court.

Now, if a 24 storey tower in Balmain comes up against problems like these, how do you think a 47 storey tower in the centre of Sydney will fare?

Of course a property development at City Tatts is all nonsense. Just get rid of Tony Guilfoyle, get the Club running properly, and then there is no need for any property development.

>Save City Tatts Committee
>Posted March 22, 2014 by savecitytatts

Bookmakers Superannuation Fund – How to recoup your losses!

Members who had money in the Bookmakers Superannuation Fund may not know, but there is provision in the superannuation legislation for a fund that has been defrauded to get financial assistance from the government.

The was intended, presumably, for where a super fund gave money to a money manager to invest who then absconded with the money.

But what the section actually says is that where a fund suffers a loss "as a result of fraudulent conduct" it can apply to the Minister for a grant of financial assistance.

Well, that's exactly what happened to the Bookmakers Superannuation Fund.

John Kennedy, and his three amigos, set up a scheme to skim .6% of every member's account every year, essentially for doing nothing. And they did this while they were the trustees of the fund. So, without a shadow of a doubt, the Bookmakers Superannuation Fund has suffered a loss 'as a result of fraudulent conduct".

Now if someone could just get Equity Trustees to apply to the Minister!
>Save City Tatts Committee
>Posted March 20, 2014 by savecitytatts

Does anybody know if Mirvac are the preferred developer?
We still don't know if Mirvac really are the "preferred developer."
We have got reports about the latest "information meeting" but instead of finding out members are more confused than ever (fairly normal for a Pat Campion meeting)
It is always good to keep in mind what experienced City Tatts watchers have told us since Tony Guilfoyle became CEO – the most important part of any meeting is what is not said.
Campion put up a slide headed "Development Management Agreement", then said "this addresses issues way beyond the scope of this meeting", and moved on to the next slide.
The Development Management Agreement, or whatever it's called, was the most important part of the meeting by far – and members learned nothing about it.
The other strange part is that nobody at the meeting could tell us for sure if the agreement was finalsed or still under negotiation.
>Save City Tatts Comittee
>Posted March 18, 2014 by savecitytatts

Did Mirvac really lose $1 billion?
People have been asking if Mirvac really wrote-off $1 billion on developments.
Yes, they did.
In February 2013 Mirvac announced a $273 million write-down on residential projects. That brought the total written-down by Mirvac for the past five years to $980 million.

By Tweedledum And Tweedledee

So much for Mirvac's "fully integrated model" that their sales rep John Carfi likes to talk about.

Although, based on those results, Mirvac's "fully integrated model" is an almost perfect match for Tony Guilfoyle's "Strategic Plan".

Posted March 16, 2014 by savecitytatts

Mirvac – 3 months and counting!

It is now three months since Patrick Campion told members that Mirvac were the "preferred developer" – and still Mirvac have said nothing.

If they really are the "preferred developer" then something is not right here. Remember that this is an industry that can't wait to trumpet any scrap of good news. Mirvac's silence can only mean that they are keeping their options open about the project.

The other issue is that Mirvac are listed on the ASX – which means they have a duty to keep shareholders informed, especially where there are significant risks involved.

Just consider the risks involved with the City Tatts deal:

The site is owned by the members of a club who can reject the project at any time. (Even a high turnout at Rookwood might not be enough to get it over the line)

The management or committee of City Tatts are liable to be under investigation by the Office of Gaming & Racing, the Independent Liquor & Gaming Authority or the Fraud Squad.

The site itself poses major construction problems.

All of the above means that any development will suffer major delays, if it ever happens. And who knows what the apartment market in Sydney will be like when Mirvac's sales campaign is ready. As Jon Chonley from Colliers put it "the sale of units is at Mirvac's risk". Indeed.

In fact, Mirvac wrote off about $1 billion on various residential projects over a period of 5 years – and that was on projects that had far less problems than the City Tatts development. Maybe the Australian Shareholders Association will take an interest in this.

>Save City Tatts Committee
>Posted March 12, 2014 by savecitytatts

Just press the buzzer at the door!
Marrickville RSL really is the future of City Tatts.
One of the hilarious details to come out of the ILGA investigation was how Marrickville RSL "operated" from an office on Marrickville Road after they sold their building to a property developer. In particular, there was no name at the front door of the office and the only way to enter was by "pressing a buzzer at the front door providing there is someone in the office to open the door".
Now that's what you call an exclusive club!
So don't be surprised if something similar happens at City Tatts. In fact, Tony Guilfoyle always had a weird fantasy in this area. He tried a few times to turn part of City Tatts into a hip nightspot like you see featured in gossip columns. Naturally, all of these attempts failed, like everything else he has tried. Still, as long as there is some kind of office he can continue to draw his salary.

>Save City Tatts Committee
>Posted March 8, 2014 by savecitytatts

One simple step to stop all the nonsense at City Tatts
Watching the Marrickville RSL saga started us thinking that there is one simple step that will stop all the nonsense at City Tatts.
One of the interesting, and amusing, details to come out of

the ILGA investigation is that the former CEO, Dalley Robinson, is now "self-representing". (He is also feeling "quite unwell" – these two details may be connected).

How does this affect City Tatts?

Well, eventually the committee of City Tatts will cut Tony Guilfoyle loose – if for no other reason than to save their own necks. (This will probably be accompanied by expressions of shock that he was doing terrible things and not telling them.) Already there are "rumblings" from a few on the committee that Guilfoyle's time is up. Now, don't misunderstand what we are saying here. It was obvious five years ago that Guilfoyle was looting the Club and he still got total support from the committee. That is why we are certain that these "rumblings" are self-preservation rather than genuine concern for the Club. But eventually he will go.

Once Tony Guilfoyle is "self-representing", instead of spending club money, all the nonsense will stop. Since he became CEO in 2004 over $1 million has been paid to Bartier Perry in legal fees. About three quarters of this was to protect Guilfoyle and the committee (ie. Guilfoyle) from members. This is a key reason why he has been able to last so long.

But if he has to pay for his defence from his own pocket – all the nonsense will stop.

  Save City Tatts Committee
  Posted March 3, 2014 by savecitytatts

$550 an hour – An administrator would be cheaper than Guilfoyle!

There is another reason to appoint an administrator to City Tatts. It would be fantastic value at $550 per hour.

Why do we say that?

Well have a look at what Tony Guilfoyle costs. He is paid about $12,000 a week and he rarely works more than 20 hours. In addition he has engaged a small army of overpaid promotion managers, chefs, maintenance supervisors and secretaries, all of whom then seem to need consultants to tell them how to do their jobs. So replacing Guilfoyle (and the hangers-on) with an administrator would mean an instant saving of at least $20,000 a week.

But that is only the start.

The administrator would be an actual expert at managing clubs, as opposed to Guilfoyle, who hasn't got a clue. And the administrator would only be paid while he was actually working for City Tatts (what a concept!). We think it would take about 6 months to stop the major rorts that have bled the Club and another 6 months to get the Club running the way it used to be. Then there would be no need for a property development.

There is another advantage of having an administrator – the powers of the City Tatts committee would cease while the administrator sorted out the Club. When an administrator is appointed, he performs the functions of the committee "to the exclusion of any other person or body of persons". In City Tatts that could only be good. Has anyone contacted the Independent Liquor & Gaming Authority?

    Save City Tatts Committee
    Posted February 25, 2014 by savecitytatts

ILGA – Please appoint an administrator to City Tatts!

The Independent Liquor & Gaming Authority (ILGA) has appointed an administrator to Marrickville RSL. The administrator will act as the governing body of the Club with immediate effect, and the current board was stripped of all powers. Why did ILGA do this?

Well here are their reasons:

They wanted an administrator to "review the Club's affairs and ensure that compliance with the (Registered Clubs) Act is now the Club's first priority".

ILGA said "given the protracted and deliberate non compliance with a fundamental requirement of the Act and noting those further instances of non compliance with regulatory matters that should have been obvious to the Club ... it is in the public interest for an insolvency professional with experience in the administration of registered clubs to ensure an independent review of the Club's affairs ..."

ILGA also said that an administrator will provide "the Club with a period of expert management and a focus on compliance that the current Board has not demonstrated. The appointment of an administrator will also indicate to the industry that, if the board of any registered club does not give appropriate priority to compliance with the Act, this Authority will appoint an administrator to take control of the club's affairs, to bring appropriate discipline to that registered club.

Well, if these are reasons for appointing an administrator, then ILGA must appoint an administrator to City Tattersalls Club. Everything that concerned them at Marrickville RSL is far worse at City Tatts. And that's without mentioning a long list of other issues that Marrickville RSL never had.

Can someone call in to ILGA and see what the steps are to appoint an administrator to City Tatts?

> Save City Tatts Committee
> Posted February 21, 2014 by savecitytatts

Marrickville RSL – the future of City Tatts?
Just finished reading the report by the Independent Liquor & Gaming Authority into Marrickville RSL. It's 24 pages and a great read. We highly recommend it.

THE DESTRUCTION OF CITY TATTERSALLS

We can't quite put a finger on it but there was something vaguely familiar about the story. Let's see now, what could it be:
* A once thriving club now on it's last legs
* A CEO who, shall we say, gave his own financial interests a higher priority than the welfare of the club
* Losses and outgoings that drained the club
* The club's situation got so bad that they "had to" sell the club's building to a property developer

A long list of breaches of the Registered Clubs Act and general corporate governance guidelines

Are you with us so far? Good, then let's continue:

The development didn't go as smoothly as planned but the club was forced to stick with the developer anyway because there was now a mortgage on the property

The CEO continued to receive his salary even though there was no club to manage

Does any of this sound familiar?

While we appreciate the efforts of ILGA in the Marrickville RSL case, we have to say that they need to get out more. What happened at Marrickville RSL is child's play compared to what goes on at City Tatts. The report talks about "huge sums" in losses and outgoings at Marrickville RSL. The sums involved are petty cash compared to the waste at City Tatts. If you counted up the money wasted on executive salaries, advertising and consultants fees, restaurant losses and botched building jobs at City Tatts for the past 10 years it would top $17 million – enough to clear the mortgage.

And as for the Marrickville RSL Secretary/Manager, Dalley Robinson, you can see why he would be a spiritual leader for any club with an insane CEO. One of his many achievements, noted in the report, was to operate the club, after the building was sold, out of a rented office – with no name on the door!

He also ensured that the club contributed to worthy community groups. We were especially amused by various payments listed as "Tara Coleman (unexplained)".

For some reason ILGA are debating whether Dalley Robinson is a fit and proper person to act as Secretary of a registered club. ILGA also reminded us that the Registered Clubs Act requires that a club "shall be conducted in good faith as a club". No doubt many club CEO's feel that is asking too much – in fact we're surprised ClubsNSW hasn't lobbied to have that requirement removed.

Dalley Robinson says he is not able to help ILGA with their enquiries because he is "feeling quite unwell". Well, with his salary gone and paying his own legal bills – yep he'd be sick alright!

       Save City Tatts Committee
       Posted February 17, 2014 by savecitytatts

Mirvac - 2 months and counting!

David Jones lodged a Pre DA submission for their Market Street property last week. Within a few days they issued a statement to the ASX, as would be expected from any company listed on the exchange.

Meanwhile, Mirvac, much further advanced on the City Tatts project (if you believe Pat Campion) have said nothing to the ASX.

This doesn't make sense.

Everyone who follows the ASX tells us that if Mirvac really are the preferred developer for a $100 million project they must inform the market. Besides, this is an industry known for insane self-promotion. They jump at any opportunity for publicity. Being nominated as preferred developer for a major site in Sydney CBD is something that the publicity department of every developer dreams about.

But Mirvac have said nothing.

One possible explanation is that Mirvac are having doubts about the project, or at least are not convinced enough to issue a positive statement to the ASX.

Finally, if Mirvac have said nothing after two months, how could the whole proposal be ready to put to members in June or July?

>Save City Tatts Committee
>Posted February 13, 2014 by savecitytatts

The Returning Officer At Tatts

There has been a bit of talk recently about employees who abuse their position of trust. It seems that the courts frown on that kind of thing, if the Katungul case is any guide.

Well, consider the strange case of Phillip Binns, the Returning Officer for all elections and ballots at City Tatts for the past few years.

Up to 2007, the New South Wales Electoral Commission was the Returning Officer for City Tatts, as it was for many clubs. Then City Tatts decided to get rid of them and change to a man called Phillip Binns. What makes this strange is that he was employed at the NSW Electoral Commission at the time and continued to be employed there while he acted as Reurning Officer for City Tatts! (He ran this business through the name of Ema Estevez.)

Wouldn't this be an abuse of his position of trust as an employee of the NSW Electoral Commission? Just think about it from the point of view of the employer – one of their employees conspires to take business away from their employer while continuing to draw wages from that employer.

Addendum B

City Tattersalls Club Rules

In the following pages are excerpts of the City Tattersalls Club Rules, as an Act of the New South Wales Parliament, of 1912.

Please take particular notice of Rule 6 which states a special Meeting of the Members must be convened for their consideration regarding any loans, etc., up to $5,500,000.

It is rather obvious that the Chairman's and Committee's resolution at the Committee Meeting in February, 2013, to Mortgage City Tattersalls Club's entire assets including the Freehold for $17,500,000, without the Members knowledge let alone addressing their legal right, was a gross act of deception, intentional or otherwise, imposed upon the Club's Members, for it was a complete disregard of Rule 6 as per the NSW Parliamentary Act of 1912.

You be the judge.

The City Tattersall's Club Act

New South Wales

ANNO TERTIO.

GEORGII V. REGIS.

* * *

·An Act to enable the members of City Tattersall's Club to alter its existing rules to sue and be sued in the name of its Chairman; and in other respects to carry out the objects of the Club.
[Assented to 3rd December, 1912.]

WHEREAS a racing and sporting club has been formed, and has for some years existed in Sydney under the name of City Tattersall's Club, and has from time to time initiated and conducted race meetings and has accumulated funds: And whereas doubts have arisen as to whether the objects of the club and powers of the committee and members thereof are sufficiently defined by the rules, and as to the method by which such rules may be legally altered or supplemented, so as to bind all the members of the said club without the express consent thereto of each and every member of the said club: And whereas the members of the said club are desirous that the said doubts should be removed and that power should be given to the majority of the members of the said club to amend the said rules: Be it therefore enacted by the King's Most Excellent Majesty, by and with the advice and consent of the Legislative Council and Legislative Assembly of New South Wales in Parliament assembled, and by the authority of the same as follows:-

Short Title.	1.	This Act may be cited for all purposes as the "City Tattersall's Club Act of 1912."
Interpretation	2.	In this Act (unless otherwise indicated by the context) -
Annually adjusted.		**Annually adjusted**, in respect of a monetary amount, means adjusted on 1 January each year in accordance with the annual percentage increase (if any) in the Consumer Price Index.
CPI.		**Consumer Price Index** means the number appearing in the Consumer Price Index (All Groups Index) for Sydney issued by the Australian Statistician.
Club.		**Club** means the said City Tattersall's Club.
Chairman.		**Chairman** means the chairman for the time being of the club.
Committee.		**Committee** means the committee for the time being of the club.
Member. Members.		**Member** and **members** mean respectively a member and members for the time being of the club.
Present Rules to be in force until adoption of new Rules.	3.	Until the passing and adopting of new rules in the manner hereinafter provided, the present rules of the club shall, so far as they are not inconsistent with this Act, be in force and binding on all the members.

Committee may call meetings for adoption of new rules or repeal or amendment of existing Rules.	4.	The Committee may, and upon the written requisition of not less than ten members, shall from time to time call meetings of the club, of which at least one month's notice shall be given, for the adoption of new rules, or the repeal or amendment of the existing rules, such meetings to be called in the same manner and subject to the same conditions as shall be provided by the rules of the club for the time being with respect to the calling of special general meetings thereof. At any such meeting of which not less than thirty members are present, the proposed new rules or repeals or amendments of existing rules shall be submitted for the consideration of the meeting, and the same may be approved, rejected, or amended by the majority of such meeting or any adjournment thereof, and upon being confirmed as hereinafter in this Act provided, shall so far as they are not inconsistent with this Act, become the rules of the club, and binding upon the members.
Chairman to Convene Meeting for Purpose of Confirming or rejecting change in Rules.	5.	After any change in the rules has been carried at any meeting of the club duly carried for that purpose the chairman shall convene another meeting of the club in the same manner as aforesaid for the purpose of confirming or rejecting such change. At any such meeting at which not less than thirty members are present, the new rules, and the repeals and amendments of the existing rules which may have been carried at the former meeting, shall be put separately to the meeting, and shall thereupon be each confirmed or rejected, but no amendments shall be allowed, and such of the new rules, repeals, or amendments as are duly confirmed by a majority of the meeting shall thereupon, so far as they are not inconsistent with this Act, be binding on all the members: Provided that any member disapproving of any change in the rules of the club may, within one calendar month of such confirmation, resign his membership, and shall thereupon be relieved from all liabilities which may by such new rules, alterations, or amendments, be imposed upon the members.
Power to Borrow or to sell or grant leases.	6.	It shall be lawful for the committee in the name of the chairman from time to time on behalf of and for the purposes of the said club, to borrow money by way of mortgage or other form of security of the lands, tenements, and hereditaments, real or personal, of the club, or by issue of debentures, secured upon the land, tenements, and hereditaments, real or personal, of the club, or in any other way upon the security of the lands, tenements, or hereditaments, real or personal, of the club, or to sell or grant leases for any term of the lands, tenements and hereditaments, real or personal, of the club, or any portion thereof, and in any way realise or dispose of the money, goods and chattels, choses in action, or other personality of the club for and in furtherance of the objects of the club: Provided that no such borrowing, mortgage, issue of debentures, or sale or leasing of the said lands, tenements and hereditaments in an amount, at one time or in one contract, exceeding $1,500,000 (annually adjusted) or in an amount, at one time or in one contract, that would result in the club's interest-bearing liabilities exceeding $5,500,000 (annually adjusted) shall be made, without the consent of the majority of a special general meeting of the club called to consider such proposed borrowing, mortgage, issue of debentures, sale, or leasing.
Power to Purchase or lease buildings or lands, and erect Club premises thereon.	7.	It shall be lawful for the committee in the name of the chairman, from time to time, on behalf of the club, to expend the funds of the club, now held by the club, or hereafter accruing or accumulating, in improving, repairing, renovating, or rebuilding the premises now occupied by the club, or in the purchase or lease of other buildings for the use of the members as club premises, or in the purchase or lease of land, and in the erection thereon of buildings for the use of the members as club premises, and in the improvement of such land and the repair or alteration of such premises; and also from time to time, in the name of the chairman, to invest the funds of the club now held by the club, or hereafter accruing or accumulating in bank deposits or Government debentures of any of the Australian States or in loan on the mortgage of real property in the City of Sydney: Provided that no such purchase or lease shall be made, and no such buildings shall be erected, and no expenditure exceeding $1,500,000 (annually adjusted) at one time or in one contract shall be made in the improvement of such land or repair or alteration of such premises, and no investment of the funds of the club exceeding $1,500,000 (annually adjusted) shall be made without the consent in each case of a majority of a special general meeting called to consider the proposed purchase, lease, erection of buildings, improvement, repair,

alteration, or investment, as the case may be.

Real and Personal Property of the Club to be vested in the Chairman

8. All lands, tenements, and hereditaments, and all personal chattels and effects which are now held by the club or by any person in trust for or on behalf of the club or the members thereof, shall immediately upon the passing of this Act become and be vested in and be held by the chairman and his successors in such office in trust for the club, and in the like manner as if such chairman and his respective successors in such office were in law a corporation sole, and if the personality were real estate, and all lands, tenements, and hereditaments, real and personal, and all personal chattels and effects which may hereafter be contracted for or be acquired by or belong to the club or the members thereof collectively may be conveyed, assigned, and assured to, and shall therefrom become vested in the chairman and his successors in such office in trust for the club, and in like manner as if such chairman and his successors in such office were in law a corporation sole, and if the personality were real estate.

Actions to be in the name of the Chairman

9. All actions, suits, proceedings, or prosecutions in any court, civil or criminal, and whether at law or in equity, commenced, instituted, prosecuted, or continued from and after the passing of this Act, by or on behalf of the club, against any person whatsoever, or against the club, whether such person be a member of the club or otherwise, shall and may be lawfully commenced, instituted, prosecuted, continued, or defended in the name of the chairman holding office at the time of the commencement of such action, suit, proceeding, or prosecution as nominal plaintiff, defendant, petitioner, respondent, or prosecutor, as the case may be, for and on behalf of the club and its members and in all indictments and informations it shall be lawful to state the property of the club to be the property of the chairman, and any offence committed with intent to injure or defraud the club may in any prosecution for the same be stated or said to have been committed with intent to defraud or injure the chairman, and the death, resignation, or removal or other act of the chairman, in whose name any such proceeding shall have been commenced, shall not abate any such action, suit, proceeding, or prosecution, but the same may be continued and concluded in the same name.

Memorial in the Chairman's name to be recorded in the Supreme Court.

10. Within one calendar month of the passing of this Act a memorial in the name of the chairman, substantially in the form set forth in the Schedule to this Act, signed by the chairman, shall be recorded upon oath, which oath any justice of the peace or commissioner for affidavits is hereby empowered to take, by the secretary of the club in the Supreme Court of New South Wales; and whenever and as often as any new chairman shall be elected, a memorial in the name of such newly-elected chairman in the same or similar form and signed by such newly-elected chairman shall, within one calendar month of the election, of such new chairman, be recorded upon oath taken as aforesaid by the secretary of the club in the Supreme Court of New South Wales, and the production in any court of justice, or before any person having by law or by consent of parties authority to hear evidence of any such memorial or any office or examined copy thereof, shall be prima facie evidence of the truth of the statements, in such memorial, or office, or examined copy, and the production in any such court or before any person having authority as aforesaid of the then last registered memorial or of any office or examined copy thereof, shall be prima facie evidence that the chairman therein named is the chairman of the club.

No action to be brought until memorial is recorded.

11. Until such memorial as hereinbefore first mentioned shall be recorded in the manner hereinbefore in this Act, directed, no action, suit, prosecution, or other proceedings shall be brought by the club or any members thereof on behalf of the club in the name of the chairman.

Effect of judgment against the Chairman.

12. Every judgment and every decree or order which shall be, at any time after the passing of this Act, obtained against the chairman on behalf of the club, shall and may take effect and be enforced and execution thereon be issued against the property and effects of the club in the same manner as if such judgment, decree, or order had been made against the said club.

Expiry of Acts

13. Expiry of Acts

    (1) This Act and the City Tattersall's Club Act Amendment Act 1936 expire on a day

ADDENDUM C

City Tattersalls Club Committee
Elected in 2013

Chairman   Patrick Campion
Vice-Chairman   Wendy Fisher
Treasurer   James Chen

Committee Members

Marytn Berry
Paul Cavallaro
Dr. Lawrence Coy
Linda Fitzhardinge
William Hurley
Kevin Smith
Michael Sterndale-Smith

Chief Executive Officer
Under contract

Anthony J. Guilfoyle

ADDENDUM E

Distribution Of Booklets
Federal Members

The Prime Minister	Tony Abbott
The Leader of the Opposition	Bill Shorten
The Attorney General	George Brandis Q.C.
Labor Party Sydney	Tanya Plibersek

State Parliament

The Premier	Barry O'Farrell
The Leader of the Opposition	Martin Ferguson
The Attorney General	Greg Smith.

The Mayor of Sydney — Clover Moore

Previous CEO — Ray Smith

The NSW State Parliamentary Members
- John Ajaka
- Richard Amery
- Kevin Anderson
- Greg Aplin
- Stuart Ayres
- Mike Baird
- John Barilaro
- Clayton Barr
- Bart Bassett
- Craig Baumann

By Tweedledum And Tweedledee

Gladys Berejiklian
Neil Blair
Peter Borsak
Stephen Bromhead
Glenn Brookes
Robert Brown
Jeremy Buckingham
Linda Burney
Cherie Burton
Charles Casuscelli
David Clarke
Rick Colless
Barry Collier
Kevin Conolly
ndrew Constance
Andrew Cornwell
Sophie Cotsis
Mark Coure
Catherine Cusack
Michael Daley
Tanya Davies
Victor Dominello
Bryan Doyle
Garry Edwards
David Elliott
Lee Evans
Mehreen Faruqi
Amanda Fazio
Marie Ficarra
John Flowers
Luke Foley
Andrew Fraser
Robert Furolo
Mike Gallacher
Jenny Gardiner
Duncan Gay

THE DESTRUCTION OF CITY TATTERSALLS

Andrew Gee
Thomas George
Melanie Gibbons
Pru Goward
Troy Grant
Alex Greenwich
Chris Gufaptis
Shelley Hancock
Chris Hartcher
Noreen Hay
Brad Hazzard
Katrina Hodgkinson
Ron Hoenig
Chris Holstein
Sonia Hornery
Kevin Humphries
Tony Issa
Matt Kean
Kristina Keneally
Nick Lalich
Geoff Lee
Paul Lynch
Daryl Maguire
Andrew McDonald
Adam Marshall
Tania Mihailuk
Bruce Notley-Smith
Jonathan Q'Dea
Barry O'Farrell
Tim Owen
Donald Page
Ryan Park
Jamie Parker
Robyn Parker
Chris Patterson
Gregory Pearce

By Tweedledum And Tweedledee

Dominic Perrottet
Barbara Perry
Peter Phelpa
Adrian Piccoli
Greg Pipe
Peter Primose
Geoff Provest
Nathan Rees
Anthony Roberts
John Robertson
Andrew Rohan
Jai Rowell
Roza Sage
Adam Searle
Walter Secord
Penny Sharpe
David Shoebridge
John Sidoti
Jilian Skinner
Greg Smith
George Souris
Mark Speakman
Chris Spence
Rob Stokes
Andrew Stoner
Carmel Tebbutt
Paul Toole
Gabrielle Upton
Mick Veitch
Lynda Voltz
Gareth Ward
Anna Watson
Darren Webber
Helen Westwood
Steve Whan
John Williams

THE DESTRUCTION OF CITY TATTERSALLS

Leslie Williams
Ray Williams
Ernest Wong
Guy Zangari

As well:

Australian Securities & investments Commission (A.S.I.C)

Office of Liquor, Gaming & Racing A.L.G.R.)

Independent Liquor & Gaming Authority (ILGA)

Clubs NSW.

The Fraud Squad

The Law Society

The Media, both TV and print.

By Tweedledum And Tweedledee

References

    City Tattersalls club- 75 Years

    City Tatteesalls Club Management

    City Tatteesalls Club Committee

    City Tatteesalls Club Members

    City Tatteesalls Club Act of 1912

    City Tatteesalls Club Rules

    Save City Tatts

    City Tatts Members forum

    City Tatts Information Desk

To keep in touch with developments behind the scenes, here are internet blogs and forums for further information. Google:

    savecitytatts.wordpress.com

    citytattsinformationdesk.wordpress.com

    citytattersallsmembers.wordpress.com

ADDENDUM F

Other Books published
by Johny Bineham

By Tweedledum And Tweedledee

The Cathar Dialogues

The lively discussions between Guillaume de Mirepoix, (Jim Callaghan's name in a previous Cathar existence) with his present spirit Guide, Henri de Nebours, which occurred over a period of nine years.

If you mind is so shut down with religious dogma, or your innate scepticism is totally iron clad, don't waste either your money, or your time, with this book.

A

Cathar Codex

This is an essential distillation of *The Cathar Dialogues* It lays out the Philosophy of Gnostic Catharism, as described by Henri de Nebours, and as taught by Dion, the greatest, yet most obscure of the Cathar mystics.

By Tweedledum And Tweedledee

Weddings A Total Guide

If you, or one of your family are considering a formal wedding, then this book is an excellent guide covering all aspects of a wedding in the Western world.

Joke book What a Laugh

Just as the title says, it is a book of classic jokes, Limericks and 'Rat' illustrations; often more naughty then not.

By Tweedledum And Tweedledee

THREE WARS A SOLDIER
A Lively Half a Life

An autobiographical account of a North Queensland lad who grew up to see Active Service in the Korean War, the Indonesian Confrontation and the Vietnam War.

www.ingramcontent.com/pod-product-compliance
Lightning Source LLC
Chambersburg PA
CBHW071759200526
45167CB00017B/514